MARTINA NAVRATILOVA

LIVES OF NOTABLE GAY MEN AND LESBIANS

MARTINA NAVRATILOVA

GILDA ZWERMAN

MARTIN DUBERMAN, General Editor

CHELSEA HOUSE PUBLISHERS ▨ New York Philadelphia

CHELSEA HOUSE PUBLISHERS

EDITORIAL DIRECTOR   Richard Rennert
EXECUTIVE MANAGING EDITOR   Karyn Gullen Browne
COPY CHIEF   Robin James
PICTURE EDITOR   Adrian G. Allen
CREATIVE DIRECTOR   Robert Mitchell
ART DIRECTOR   Joan Ferrigno
MANUFACTURING DIRECTOR   Gerald Levine

LIVES OF NOTABLE GAY MEN AND LESBIANS
SENIOR EDITOR   Sean Dolan
SERIES DESIGN   Basia Niemczyc

Staff for **MARTINA NAVRATILOVA**
ASSISTANT EDITOR   Annie McDonnell
PICTURE RESEARCHER   Villette Harris
COVER ILLUSTRATION   Bonnie Gardner

Introduction © 1994 by Martin B. Duberman.

First Printing

1   3   5   7   9   8   6   4   2

Library of Congress Cataloging-in-Publication Data

Zwerman, Gilda.
Martina Navratilova/Gilda Zwerman; Martin Duberman, general editor.
p. cm.—(Lives of notable gay men and lesbians)
Includes bibliographical references and index.
ISBN 0-7910-2303-6
        0-7910-2878-X (pbk.)
1. Navratilova, Martina, 1956– —Juvenile literature. 2. Tennis players—United States—Biography—Juvenile literature. 3. Lesbians—United States—Biography—Juvenile literature. [1. Navratilova, Martina, 1956–
2. Tennis players. 3. Lesbians—Biography. 4. Women—Biography.] I. Duberman, Martin B. II. Title. III. Series.
GV994.N38Z94 1995   94-23326
796.342'092'4—dc20   CIP
[B]   AC

Frontispiece
Martina Navratilova hoists the winner's trophy at the Eastbourne Championships tournament in Eastbourne, England, in June 1989.

CONTENTS

Titles in
▨ LIVES OF NOTABLE GAY MEN AND LESBIANS ▨

On Being Different

by *Martin Duberman*

Being different is never easy. Especially in a culture like ours, which puts a premium on conformity and equates difference with deficiency. And especially during the teenage years when one feels desperate for acceptance and vulnerable to judgment. If you are taller or shorter than average, or fatter or thinner, or physically challenged, or of the "wrong" color, gender, religion, nationality, or sexual orientation, you are likely to be treated as "less than," as inferior to what the majority has decreed is the optimal, standard model.

Theoretically, those of us who are different should be delighted that we are *not* ordinary, not just another cookie-cutter product of mainstream culture. We should glory in the knowledge that many remarkably creative figures, past and present, lived outside accepted norms and pressed hard against accepted boundaries.

But in reality many of us have internalized the majority's standards of worth, and we do not feel very good about ourselves. How could we?

When we look around us, we see that most people in high places of visibility, privilege, and power are white, heterosexual males of a very traditional kind. That remains true even though intolerance may have ebbed *somewhat* in recent decades and people of diverse backgrounds may have *begun* to attain more of a foothold in our culture.

Many gay men and lesbians through time have looked and acted like "ordinary" people and could therefore choose to "stay in the closet" and avoid social condemnation—though the effort at concealment produced its own turmoil and usually came at the price of self-acceptance. On the other hand, "sissy" gay men or "butch" lesbians have been quickly categorized and scorned by the mainstream culture as "sexual deviants"—even though no necessary link exists between gender nonconformity and sexual orientation. In the last 15 years or so, however, more and more people who previously would have passed as straight *have* been choosing to "come out." They sense that social consequences are no longer as severe as they once were—and that the psychic costs of concealment are taking too great a toll.

Yet even today, there are comparatively few role models available for gays and lesbians to emulate. And unlike other oppressed minorities, homosexuals don't often find confirmation within their own families. Even when a homosexual child is not rejected outright, acceptance comes within a family unit that is structurally heterosexual and in which homosexuality is generally mocked and decried. With his or her different desire and experience, the gay son or lesbian daughter remains an exotic. Moreover, such children are unable to find in family lore and traditions—as other minority people can—a compensatory source of validation to counterbalance the ridicule of mainstream culture.

Things are rarely any better at school, where textbooks and lessons are usually devoid of relevant information about homosexuality. Nor does the mainstream culture—movies or television, for example—often provide gays or lesbians with positive images of themselves, let alone any sense of historical antecedents. These silences are in large measure a reflection of the culture's homophobia. But to a lesser degree they reflect two other matters as well: the fact that many accomplished gay men and lesbians in the past refused to publicly acknowledge their sexuality (sometimes even to themselves); and secondly, the problem of assigning "gay" or "lesbian" identities to past figures who lived at a time when those conceptual categories did not exist.

For the surprising finding of recent scholarship is that categorizing human beings on the basis of sexual desire alone is a relatively recent phenomenon of the last several hundred years. It is a development, many historians believe, tied to the increasing urbanization of Europe and the Americas, and to the new opportunities city life presented for anonymity—for freedom from the relentless scrutiny of family and neighbors that had characterized farming communities and small towns. Only with the new freedom afforded by city life, historians are telling us, could people who felt they were different give free rein to their natures, lay claim to a distinctive identity, and begin to elaborate a subculture that would reflect it.

Prior to, say, 1700 (the precise date is under debate), the descriptive categories of "straight" or "gay" were not widely employed in dividing up human nature. Even today, in many non-Western parts of the world, it is unusual to categorize people on the basis of sexual orientation alone. Through time and across cultures it has often been assumed that *both* same- and opposite-gender erotic feelings (what we now call "bisexuality") could coexist in an individual—even if *acting* on same-gender impulses was usually taboo.

In the West, where we *do* currently divide humanity into oppositional categories of "gay" and "straight," most people grow up accepting that division as "natural" and dutifully assign themselves to one category or the other. Those who adopt the definition "gay" or "lesbian," however, soon discover that mainstream culture offers homosexuals (unlike heterosexuals) no history or sense of forebears. This is a terrible burden, especially during the teenage years, when one is actively searching for a usable identity, for a continuum in which to place oneself and lay claim to a contented and productive life.

This series is designed, above all, to fill that huge, painful cultural gap. It is designed to instill not only pride in antecedents but encouragement, the kind of encouragement that literature and biography have always provided: proof that someone else out there has felt what we have felt, experienced what we have experienced, been where we have been—and has endured, achieved, and flourished.

But *who* to include in this series has been problematic. Even today, many people refuse to define themselves as gay or lesbian. In some cases, they do not wish to confine what they view as their fluid sexuality into narrow, either/or categories. In other cases, they may acknowledge to themselves that their sexuality does fit squarely within the "gay" category, yet refuse to say so publicly, unwilling to take on the onus of a lesbian or gay identity. In still other cases, an individual's sense of sexual identity can change during his or her lifetime, as can his or her sense of its importance, when compared with many other strands, in defining their overall temperament.

Complicating matters still further is the fact that even today—when multitudes openly call themselves gay or lesbian, and when society as a whole argues about gay marriage and parenting or the place of gay people in the military—there is still no agreed-upon definition of what centrally constitutes a gay or lesbian identity. Should we call someone gay if his or her sexual desire is *predominantly* directed toward people of their own gender? But then how do we establish predominance? And by "desire" do we mean actual behavior—or fantasies that are never acted out? (Thus Father John McNeill, the writer and Jesuit, has insisted—though he has never actually had sex with another man—that on the basis of his erotic fantasies, he *is* a gay man.)

Some scholars and theorists even argue that genital sexuality need not be present in a relationship before we can legitimately call it gay or lesbian, stressing instead the central importance of same-gender *emotional* commitment. The problem of definition is then further complicated when we include the element of *self*-definition. If we come across someone in the past who does not explicitly self-identify as gay, by what right, and according to what evidence, can we claim them anyway?

Should we eliminate all historical figures who lived before "gay" or "lesbian" were available categories for understanding and ordering their experience? Are we entitled, for the purposes of this series, to include at least some of those from the past whose sexuality seems not to have been confined to one gender or the other, or who—as a cover, to protect a public image or a career—may have married, and thus have been commonly taken to be heterosexual? And if we do not include some of those whose sexuality cannot be clearly categorized as "gay," then how can we speak of a gay and lesbian continuum, a *history*?

In deciding which individuals to include in *Notable Gay Men and Lesbians,* I have gone back and forth between these competing definitions, juggling, combining, and, occasionally, finessing them. For the most part, I have tried to confine my choices to those figures who *by any definition* (same-gender emotional commitment, erotic fantasy, sexual behavior, *and* self-definition) do clearly qualify for inclusion.

But alas, we often lack the needed intimate evidence for such clear-cut judgments. I have regretfully omitted from the series many bisexual figures, and especially the many well-known women—Tallulah Bankhead, Judy Garland, Greta Garbo, or Josephine Baker, for example—whose erotic and emotional preference seem indeterminable (usually for lack of documentation). But I will also include a few —Margaret Mead, say, or Marlene Dietrich—as witnesses to the difficult ambiguities of sexual definition, and to allow for a discussion of those ambiguities.

In any case, I suspect much of the likely criticism over this or that choice will come from those eager to conceal their distaste for a series devoted to "Notable (no less!) Gay Men and Lesbians" under the guise of protesting a single inclusion or omission within it. That kind of criticism can be easily borne, and is more than compensated for, by the satisfaction of acquainting today's young gays and lesbians—and indeed all who feel "different"—with knowledge of some of those distinguished forebears whose existence can inform and comfort them.

❖   ❖   ❖

This biography of Martina Navratilova comes at a crucial juncture in her life. Recently retired from the world of professional tennis in which she was for so long a dominant figure, approaching forty, co-author of a mystery novel, sometime participant in gay politics, she has yet to define a firm next step for herself.

This is a time, in other words, when Martina herself is taking stock, and when the public is taking stock of Martina. And thus the special value of Gilda Zwerman's book. A subtle and penetrating study, it presents us with the opportunity to ponder the life of a woman who is all at once determined, loyal and generous—and yet capable of leaving behind previously intense commitments, personal or political, with a swiftness that has opened her up to the charge of being shallow. Beyond biography, Zwerman's book situates Martina's life within the broader cultural dynamics of the professionalization of women's sports and changing conventional definitions of femininity.

The Martina Navratilova story spans several continents. Brought up in Czechoslovakia, she lived as a youngster under the boot of the Soviet Union, yet appears to have been comfortable and happy within her own family. On the municipal tennis courts of Prague, Martina demonstrated at an early age her extraordinary zest and talent for sports. By the time she defected from Czechoslovakia in 1976 at the age of 19, she had already risen to the front ranks of players in women's tennis. Thereafter, the story becomes one of sustained dominance of the sport until, at the point of her retirement in 1994, she was being widely heralded as the "greatest woman tennis player of all time."

Martina's personal story is no less dramatic. And in recounting this side of her life, Zwerman has provided a complex portrait. In 1993 Martina said in an interview that she had defected from Czechoslovakia "about three months after I realized I was gay. I knew I couldn't be gay in Czechoslovakia"—though career considerations were of course prominent motivating factors as well.

But Martina had not always been willing to talk so openly about her sexual orientation—understandably, in a sports world in which homophobia was (and remains) rampant. As Zwerman cogently writes, "to be the ultimate success, a player had to have the right look, the right clothes, the right hair-do, the right mannerisms and the right lifestyle." With her strong, muscular body, her accented speech and no-nonsense ways, Martina had difficulty fitting the prescribed image of a "woman tennis player"; to have come out as a lesbian on top of that might have seriously compromised her career.

Zwerman explores Martina's lesbian relationships with the detailed candor they warrant—but rarely receive. Her involvements with Sandra Haynie, Rita Mae Brown, Nancy Lieberman, and Judy Nelson are examined on multiple levels, as episodes of personal history, as gay partnerships, and as revelations of Martina's character. What becomes clear in this biography is that although Martina chose throughout most of her tennis career to remain silent about her sexuality, she did so for prudential reasons—not because she felt guilty or self-hating about her love for women. Indeed, she seems always to have been accepting of herself, and of her sexuality, as something entirely natural.

The sports establishment, and the press, have been far less accepting. The press mercilessly pursued Martina and her partners, eager to pry into personal details of their relationships yet at the same time failing to treat them with respect. Even some of Martina's fellow tennis players made homophobic remarks about her—usually behind her back. And corporate sponsors largely stayed away from Martina, offering her far fewer product endorsements than an athlete of her stature would have otherwise received. But in recent years especially, Martina has refused to be daunted by her detractors, has explicitly and publicly avowed her lesbianism, and has made herself available, on an occasional basis, to do work in the lesbian and gay community.

Martina's process of "coming out" is ongoing—as it is for most gays and lesbians. The extent to which she decides to involve herself further in protest politics remains to be seen. But the mere fact of her *being* out—one of the few major sports figures ever to declare their homosexuality openly—has already proven a significant boon to the cause of lesbian and gay rights.

BEING THE BEST

Gilda Zwerman

How am I going to tell them?" she fretted. "It's not like they think homosexuality is wrong or anything. I know they support gay rights. But I think that they'll be upset when they learn it's me they're supporting."

In 1990, I was seeing a young woman in my therapy practice. Ann was 19 years old, a sophomore at a City College, living with her parents in the Bronx. Sex was chief among the topics of concern. During that year, as she socialized with both men and women, Ann had started to recognize that she felt more attracted to women. But she was afraid to "come out" to her parents.

I asked Ann if there were any circumstances under which she could imagine telling her parents that she thought she might be gay. At first she just shook her head no. Then a smile appeared on her face and she broke into a giggle. "This is going to sound completely stupid," she said, covering her face in embarrassment, "but sometimes I have this day dream, about going into a gay bar, meeting Martina Navratilova, we fall in love at first sight, and I take her on the D train up to the Bronx, open the door and say, 'Mom, Dad, I'd like you to meet my new girlfriend, Martina.' I think that would make it okay."

I jotted down the name "Martina" in my notepad so that I would remember the daydream Ann had related.

In 1990, I knew nothing about tennis. I probably could not have picked Martina Navratilova out of a lineup. My world as an academic, psychotherapist, and aging political activist was completely detached from the world of professional sports. However, later that year, while flipping channels on the television, I accidently caught a glimpse of this woman who, for Ann, was the link between her homosexuality and her self-esteem, the woman who made it all right to be gay.

There she was. Standing 5 feet 7 inches tall, blond hair, trim, muscular, a well-chiseled face wrapped in a lavender headband. Beyond the sum of her features, Martina had a distinct look that was hard to put into words—clearly female, but not frilly and willing to compromise her athleticism for the conventions of femininity. Even to a sports dunce like myself, the woman *was* impressive. Actually, both women players were impressive.

It was the women's final at Wimbledon. Martina's opponent, Zina Garrison, was the first black woman to compete in a Wimbledon final since Althea Gibson had won the title in 1958. At 33, Martina was playing for a record ninth Wimbledon title. Over the years, Garrison and Navratilova had faced each other 28 times: Martina had won 27 of those matches. Exuding confidence, Martina beat Garrison this day as well, requiring just two sets and 75 minutes to do so.

Following match point, Martina threw her arms into the air, climbed over the net to put an arm around Garrison, and then dropped to her knees. Martina Navratilova had just become Wimbledon's all-time singles champion, surpassing the record of eight singles titles she had shared with Helen Wills Moody, the player ranked number one in women's tennis from 1927 to 1938.

Then came the most dramatic moment of all. Martina rose and started for the stands. She climbed several tiers of bleachers toward the friends' box, where the competitors' special guests are seated. In front of thousands of people in the stadium and millions watching on television, Martina threw her arms around her companion of six years, Judy Nelson. The two women embraced and cried tears of delight over Martina's victory.

During the next few years, I, along with the entire country, would hear quite a bit from and about Martina—and not just in the sports section. Still playing pro tennis, Martina was becoming a champion off the courts as well. Though she had never denied her sexual orientation, in 1991 Martina took an even more courageous step. In the midst of a stormy breakup with Nelson, she came out of the closet. "I am gay," she proclaimed in a nationally televised interview with Barbara Walters. "Americans say they want honesty. Well there it is." Until that moment, no sports figure and very few celebrities of her standing had ever been willing to say those words publicly.

Since then Martina has offered her name, her time, and her money to many high-profile campaigns for gay rights. She was a plaintiff in the American Civil Liberties Union (ACLU) lawsuit contesting Amendment 2, which would have permitted discrimination against homosexuals in her home state of Colorado. She has written on behalf of the National Gay and Lesbian Task Force in order to raise money for their campaign to end the ban on gays in the military. She has done promotional work for Gay Games IV, a sports event that was held in New York City in the summer of 1994. And before a crowd of 500,000 at the Gay Rights March in Washington, D.C., in 1993, she made a powerful, personal plea for all lesbians and gay men to do exactly what she did: to come out of the closet. "By coming out to our friends, family, employers and employees, we make ourselves personal, touchable, real. We become human beings, and then we have the opportunity to show the world what we are all about—happy, intelligent, giving, loving people."

Unbeknownst to my patient Ann, I, too, became an admirer of Martina's. My appreciation of Martina is not just as a tennis champion or even a gay rights activist but as a woman who made a not-so-easy climb to the top. Leaving high school, her family, and her homeland of Czechoslovakia at the age of 18, Martina was forced to invent a life—to make a place for herself on the women's tennis tour, to learn English, to battle the Communist bureaucrats who sought to restrict her career, to construct a support system of friends, trainers, coaches, and financial managers, and to carry on intimate relationships away from the eye of the public. By 1978, at the age of 22, Martina was ranked the number-one tennis player in the world. She held that ranking in 1979 and then for five consecutive years, from 1982–86. On the court, Martina was the best there ever was. Off the court, she used her stature as the best in tennis to help redefine what being a woman and a lesbian is all about.

CHAPTER ONE

A WILLFUL, RESILIENT LITTLE GIRL

Martina Navratilova was born Martina Subertova on October 18, 1956, in Prague, the capital city of Czechoslovakia. At the time of her birth, Czechoslovakia, a relatively new nation whose history as an independent republic dated only to 1918, was oppressed by a sense of what its inhabitants called *litost,* meaning sadness or loss. What was being mourned was the belief that the nation was free to control its own destiny.

As a republic, Czechoslovakia had enjoyed one of the most liberal constitutions in the world, and the nation had prospered under the leadership of two extraordinarily able presidents, Tomas Masaryk and Edouard Beneš. But Czechoslovakia had the members of many ethnic and national minorities living within its borders, including Germans, Poles, and Hungarians. With the rise in Germany in the 1930s of the Nazi dictator Adolf Hitler, many Germans in Czechoslovakia, particularly in the western regions known as the Sudetenland, became outspoken in their desire to join

Residents of Prague demonstrate their support for the coup that swept the Communists to power in Czechoslovakia in 1948. During Navratilova's childhood, however, many Czechs were disillusioned by the Communists' failure to fulfill their promises.

Germany as part of Hitler's so-called Third Reich (empire). Their desire accorded with Hitler's wish to expand Germany's borders, and by 1938 he was declaring his intention to take the Sudetenland. Eager to avoid war, the other major powers of Europe persuaded Czechoslovakia to "appease" Hitler by giving him what he wanted. Poland and Hungary soon made similar claims for Czechoslovakian territory where Poles and Hungarians resided in large numbers, and the European powers responded similarly. By November 1938, Czechoslovakia had lost territories inhabited by almost 5 million people.

Hitler, however, was not satisfied, and on March 14, 1939, his armies invaded the rest of Czechoslovakia. The nation had become the first casualty of World War II. While Beneš worked in exile for Czechoslovakia's independence, the nation did not regain any real measure of freedom until 1945, when the Soviet Union's forces drove the Germans out.

Grateful for its liberation, Czechoslovakia found itself, perhaps inevitably, closely tied to its liberators. A Communist nation, the Soviet Union had emerged victorious from the war as the most powerful state in Europe. Faced with the task of postwar rebuilding, Czechoslovakia naturally looked to the Soviets for military and economic aid. Meanwhile, looking to expand its areas of influence and control in Eastern Europe, the Soviet Union did all that it could to ensure that Communists occupied places of importance in postwar Czechoslovakia, promising the Czechs all the while that they would be able to fashion their own brand of communism, which would combine the best of their democratic traditions with the virtues of a socialist economy. As Czech Communists had been in the forefront of the nation's liberation movement, the party could also call on considerable popular support among the Czech people. Though Beneš returned to the presidency, in 1946 the Communist Party of Czechoslovakia (KPC) received a plurality of the votes—38 percent—in a free election. Using strong-arm tactics, the Communists then forced their political opponents from the government and outlawed opposition parties. By 1948 their control of the government was virtually absolute, and Beneš resigned rather than approve a new constitution.

In the years following its ascent to power, the KPC consolidated its power. It ran the government, steered the economy, directed education, monopolized the mass media, and censored literature. Desirable jobs were meted out only to KPC loyalists. Political opposition became a criminal act, and the offense was defined very broadly.

A challenge to the KPC was a challenge to the Soviet Union as well, as the citizens of Czechoslovakia learned the year that Navratilova was born. In neighboring Hungary, another in the "bloc" of Eastern European nations that had acquiesced to Communist rule after World War II, a move toward liberalization was taking place, an attempt to create a "third road" between communism and capitalism. With demonstrations in favor of free elections and independence spreading throughout the country, the Soviets responded with force. Soviet troops mercilessly crushed the rebellion in a matter of weeks. Thousands of Hungarians were killed in the fighting; thousands more were jailed and executed, and 80,000 Soviet troops were stationed in the country to discourage further upheaval.

The consequences of opposition could not have been made clearer to the people of Czechoslovakia, who were now made to realize, if they had not earlier, that their liberators had become their captors. A sense of individual freedom, no less than national independence, had been lost. Most Czechs did what they were told and carried out the government's orders, but they searched for ways to enjoy moments of freedom—in their personal lives, in recreation, and in nature.

Martina Subertova's family was independent-minded: obedient on the outside, critical on the inside. Her mother, Jana Semanska, had been raised on a large estate in the Brdy Mountains, high above the village of Revnice, about 16 miles from Prague. Her family owned 30 acres of lush farmland covered with apple trees, berry bushes, and wild mushrooms. After the accession of the Communists, who opposed the accumulation of private property, the estate was divided up, leaving Martina's grandparents with a tiny one-room apartment on the top floor of the house they had once owned.

Jana had married Mirek Subert, a restaurant manager from Prague, in the early 1950s. Soon after, Mirek took a job as a patroller for a ski lodge, Martinovka, which was located in the snow-capped Krkonose Mountains. When the couple had their first child in 1956, they decided to give her a feminized version of the name of the ski lodge where she had been conceived.

Martina spent her early childhood on the slopes of the Krkonose Mountains, where she learned to ski almost as soon as she learned to

walk. At age two, barely out of diapers, her athletic skills were already evident. Later she could even recall the pleasure she felt whizzing down a hill for the first time, with the snow under her skis and the sun in her eyes. "I was a happy little kid," she said in *Martina: An Autobiography*, which she wrote with sportswriter George Vecsey and was published in 1985.

In February 1948, huge crowds filled the streets of Prague to demonstrate their support for the Communist party's bid to take a greater share of the power in the Czech government. Initially, many Czechs supported the Communists in the belief that they would bring a greater degree of economic and social equality to Czech society.

Her parents, however, were not so happy, at least not with each other. Jana and Mirek separated when Martina was three. With her daughter, Jana moved back in with her parents at Revnice. With four people cramped in one room, no hot water, no car, and very little money, conditions there were difficult. Adding to the difficulty was the growing mental instability of Martina's grandfather, who was sometimes abusive, sometimes paranoid, and always carried around a large ring of keys, which he used to constantly lock and unlock doors. As a young child, Martina recalled in her autobiography, she felt that things in her life were not quite right: "Somehow I had the sense of things being out of focus, out of place, the sense that I should be somewhere else." She had inherited her family's and her nation's indignant attitude toward the government. She understood that although her family had a little more freedom and money than many other Czechs, they had also lost more than others had. She would stare out of the window at a grove of apple trees that used to belong to her grandparents, knowing they had been given to someone else by the Communist authorities.

Martina's estrangement from her father was another source of sadness and confusion in her childhood. After her parents separated, she occasionally visited her father at the ski lodge. Once in a while he came to Revnice on the weekend and took her to the Prague Zoo. But over time, their visits became less frequent and eventually stopped, and he became a distant and shadowy figure in her life. Martina was told that her father had become ill, with a stomach ailment. He died when she was seven, but she was not told that he was dead until she was eleven. Much later in life, Martina would discover other disturbing facts about her father: that he had not died of an illness but had killed himself and that he had fathered a son before meeting Jana.

Martina felt safest with her "Mami," as she called her mother. Intelligent, capable, and resilient, Jana served as a strong role model for her daughter. As soon as her day of work in a factory was over, she returned home to cook meals for her young daughter. In the evening, she read and studied languages on her own. Whenever possible, she played tennis or went skiing, always taking Martina along with her.

It was on the municipal tennis courts that Jana met the man who would become her next husband and Martina's new father. Actually, Martina met him first. One day in early spring, four-year-old Martina was amusing herself by following a maintenance crew around the grounds while her mother played tennis. She took a special liking to one of the men who was repairing the courts. Mirek Navratil responded affectionately to the skinny little pip-squeak who stood willfully, her arms folded, in front of his wheelbarrow, demanding that he give her a ride. Relenting, he threw her into the empty cart and pushed her around, making her laugh. They became fast friends. Later, when Jana met this man on her own, Mirek was pleased to learn the little girl he had already "adopted" was Jana's daughter.

Soon Mirek was spending time at the house with Martina and her mother. Jana was happy and relieved to have a man around, and since Mirek and Martina had already established a relationship independent of Martina's mother, Martina did not seem to experience the usual jealousy a child often feels when her single mother gets involved with a "new" man. After all, Martina had picked him out.

Mirek and Jana married in 1961. When they came back from their honeymoon, Martina started calling Mirek "Tato," a variation of Daddy. After Martina's biological father died, Mirek adopted her. In the Czech language, every girl takes the feminine ending "ova" after her father's family name. If she later marries, she takes the same ending after her husband's family name. When she was 10, Martina's last name was changed from Subertova to Navratilova.

Jana's new husband moved in with her and her daughter in the room they shared with Martina's grandparents. Two years later, Martina's sister, Jana, was born. The apartment was terribly crowded, but Mirek's presence and the arrival of a new baby lightened the mood of the household. When the apartment downstairs became vacant, the Navratils moved in. Like Jana, Mirek enjoyed life, enjoyed sports, and valued personal freedom. He worked as an economist in a factory but refused to join the KPC, a refusal that cost him a lifetime of promotions and pay increases. He rode to and from work on a motorcycle. He spent most of his leisure time with his family. They skied and swam and picked berries and mushrooms together; they gardened and cooked. The family even managed to save enough money to take a vacation during the summer.

For Martina, Mirek was not only "Tato" but a close companion and teacher. He encouraged her to participate in all kinds of sports, including soccer and ice hockey, with little regard for whether she played against boys or girls. Martina loved the attention and loved the activity. Never much for playing indoors or with dolls, Martina tended to choose friends, such as her companions Eva Pekarkova and Kveta Vlaskova, who enjoyed active games and being outdoors as much as she did.

Fast on her feet, well-balanced, well-coordinated, skinny, and muscular, Martina seemed to be naturally well suited for athletics. Mirek called her *prut,* or stick, because of her skin-and-bones figure. In the United States, young Martina might have been called a "tomboy," but one of the more positive aspects of the Communist system was a regard for women and girls as equal to their male counterparts. Czech women were encouraged to do everything that the men did, in both the workplace and in recreational activities. Thus, Martina's aptitude for athletics was encouraged and nurtured, first by her family and later by the government.

Although she preferred to be running around, Martina was a good student who managed without much effort to get grades that were well above average. Her best subjects were language, literature, and mathematics. The ease with which she learned new material and absorbed information made her somewhat cocky, and she was known to talk out of turn and clown around in the classroom. Sometimes she would keep her hand raised in the air through an entire lesson, just to let everyone know that she knew all the answers. Martina tempered her attitude and conduct in each class according to her feelings about the teacher: if the teacher was fair-minded and had interesting things to say, Martina followed the rules. If the teacher was arbitrary and authoritarian, Martina made his or her life difficult. In either case, by the time she reached the sixth grade, schoolwork had definitely taken a backseat to the emergent passion in her life: tennis.

When Czechoslovakia emerged as an independent and relatively prosperous nation in the early part of the 20th century, the Czech middle class embraced the game of tennis as a recreational pastime. Martina's grandfather had built a red clay tennis court on the grounds of his estate. Although much of the property had been reapportioned by the Communists, the now–run-down court had remained in the family's possession.

The first tennis racket that Martina held in her hands had belonged to her grandmother, Agnes Semanska. Both she and Martina's mother had been avid tennis players. In fact, Agnes Semanska had once played and defeated the grandmother of Helena Sukova (a future rival of Martina's on the professional tour) in a Czech national tournament.

The racket was old-fashioned, made of wood, with a little crooked head and no tape on the grip. While her parents were playing recreational tennis at the municipal club, Martina would stand near the wall behind the last court, hold the racket in both hands, and hit the ball against the wall. In a short time she was pounding the ball and was able to maintain a volley with herself for minutes on end.

When Mirek heard the sound of the ball against the back wall, he was struck by Martina's consistency and strength. She was not yet even six years old. In her autobiography, Martina remembered the first time Mirek led her away from the wall and onto a real tennis court: "The moment I stepped onto that crunchy red clay, felt the grit under my sneakers, felt the joy of smacking a ball over the net, I knew I was in the right place. . . . Mirek was at the net and I was between the service line and the baseline. I could have hit with him all day. I had all the energy and all the patience in the world."

From then on, Martina played tennis every day, from the time the snow melted in the spring until it returned in the fall. Mirek repaired the tennis court on their property, and both parents practiced with her. Soon she started to beat her mother regularly. There were also tennis courts across the street from Martina's school: she would play on them after school and daydream about playing on them during class.

When Martina was eight, Mirek entered her in her first junior tournament. The competition took place 30 miles from Revnice, so the two traveled there on Mirek's motorcycle. Mirek was so certain that Martina would lose in one of the early matches that he failed to bring enough money for meals. By the time his daughter had advanced to the semifinals, they were subsisting on potatoes and cream cheese, the cheapest items on the local menus.

Martina's self-image as a future tennis pro was solidified on the night Mirek took her to Sparta Sports Arena in Prague to watch Rod Laver, the internationally known Australian tennis champion who would make his mark as one of the greatest champions of all time. As soon as she saw this redheaded left-hander rocketing around the court, Martina recalled in her autobiography, she thought, "That's it, that's me, that's the player I want to be." She began having dreams about winning on Centre Court at Wimbledon, where the All-England Lawn Tennis and Croquet Club holds its annual tournament, the most prestigious in the world. Even KPC officials had great respect for the tradition of Wimbledon and supported young Czechs who showed promise as potential competitors in this tournament. "It was one dream you were allowed to have," explained Martina.

Mirek also recognized that this dream would fuel Martina's drive and inspire her to develop her skills. "Make believe you're at Wimbledon, hold up your trophy," he would say after a morning on the courts. Mirek always tried to make practicing tennis fun for Martina, but soon he knew that it was time to get his daughter some serious training.

Like everything else in Communist Czechoslovakia, tennis training was controlled and directed by the government, in this case by an administrative body called the Czech Tennis Federation. The federation funneled its top prospects into ten regional training centers, from which the best ultimately emerged for further development at a national center in Prague. Czech coaches were among the best in the world; those with the highest certificates had studied physiology and psychology and even earned a master's degree in the theory of sport. The Czech Tennis Federation paid the coaches, offered free lessons to talented players, and partially underwrote travel expenses to tournaments.

The Australian Rocket, Rod Laver (seen here competing at the U.S. Open in 1959), was one of Navratilova's first inspirations as a tennis player.

In her autobiography Martina described her first encounter with George Parma, a former Czech Davis Cup champion and her first coach. "How old is he?" Parma asked Mirek on first seeing his would-be pupil, deceived by her short hair and wiry build. The meeting took place at Klamovka Park, a tiny tennis emporium that was the only facility in Prague with three indoor courts. The best one was heated, but the others were so cold that sometimes players would have to wear a hat and gloves. He was very busy, the coach told Mirek, and had only a few hours to spend on new players. He could not promise anything.

Then he began to hit balls at Martina, who was wearing a little burgundy warm-up suit and carrying a secondhand racket. "I think we can do something with her," he said after half an hour.

George Parma became Martina's inspiration and idol. After just a few lessons, she "would have walked through fire for this tall, handsome man," as she put it in her autobiography. "He was like a god to me—cool, intelligent, well-educated. He had travelled outside Czechoslovakia many times and knew five languages. . . . He was patient and never shouted or downgraded me. . . . I was so excited to work with him that I'd chase down every ball until I ran out of breath."

Parma trained Martina to be a "serve and volley" player, a style that is more aggressive, riskier, and takes longer to perfect than the "baseline" manner of play adopted by most female players. As a result, it was likely that it might take longer for Martina to perfect her game than other players, but she could also expect to compete successfully past the age when most female players retire.

In addition to playing tennis and being coached by Parma, there was another attraction for Martina in Prague. When the trip back and forth from Revnice to the city became too tiring, especially when she had lessons on both Friday afternoon and Saturday morning, she spent the night at the apartment of her paternal grandmother, Andela Subertova.

Grandma Subertova's apartment was small, just one bedroom and a kitchen–living room area, where she would fix up a couch into a bed for Martina. After she made dinner with lunch meat or chicken and carrot salad, she and her granddaughter would sit around and talk and tell jokes all evening or listen to music or do crossword puzzles. To Grandma Subertova, Martina was "Zlata Holcika," her little "golden girl." For Martina, Grandma Subertova was the person who gave her love unconditionally. "She was the voice of approval that I always heard in the back of my mind, the person who loved me whether or not I had a good day at the tennis courts or finished my homework or cleaned my room," she recalled in her autobiography.

At first Martina's tennis lessons were not so different from the instruction on the piano or in German that she also received. There were no exceptions made for her in school, and when she was not at Klamovka Park she kept up with family and friends. But as the true extent of her interest and skill revealed itself, priorities shifted. More and more of her time and energy and of the family's resources were devoted to her tennis.

The Navratils gave up their vacations so that Martina could play in tournaments. They had to fill out tournament applications, keep track of schedules, and transport her to local matches. When tournaments were held in other cities, Mirek would accompany Martina. A player did not get reimbursed for expenses until she won the first match, so the two would pack up food rations before setting off on Mirek's motorcycle.

Eventually, Martina went to tournaments on her own, staying with local families who were involved in the junior tournament circuit. By age 10, Martina was aware that she was special: her athletic ability set her apart from her peers, and her future would be different from theirs.

CHAPTER TWO

THIS FUTURE
IS NOT FOR ME

On Wednesday, August 21, 1968, Martina was scheduled to play in a junior tournament in the town of Pilsen. She arrived the day before and spent the night in the home of her doubles partner, Vera Hrdinova. The two girls stayed up late, giggling and talking. At about six o'clock the next morning, the phone rang. It was Vera's father, calling from work to tell her and Martina to remain in the house. Overnight, the streets outside had been lined with soldiers and armored tanks from the Soviet Union and five other Eastern European Communist nations.

The Russian occupation came in response to the growing liberalization and reform movement in Prague. In January 1968, Alexander Dubcek replaced Anton Novotny as first secretary of the KPC, the most important party position. Two months later, Novotny was also forced to resign the nation's presidency, in favor of Ludvik Svoboda. While Novotny had a reputation for being even more repressive than the Rus-

As premier of the Czech Communist party, Alexander Dubcek tried to navigate a middle course between his countrymen's demands for greater freedom and the Soviet Union's insistence on stricter political and social control.

sians themselves, Svoboda was a critic of the Communist coup in 1948. Though a firm believer in communism, Dubcek believed that its ideals had been corrupted by the leaders of the Soviet Union and Czechoslovakia.

For the first time in 20 years, the Czech people had reason to hope that their basic democratic rights would be restored. Dubcek promised to amend the constitution to guarantee freedom of speech and assembly, to curtail censorship, to grant Czechs the right to travel abroad, to institute a program of reimbursement for property that had been forcibly seized by the state (such as Martina's grandparents' estate), and to allow political participation by non-KPC members. According to Dubcek, such reforms were not intended as a rejection of communism but as a fulfillment of the original promise the Communists had made to the Czech people in 1948—to build "socialism with a human face."

August 20, 1968, was one of the darkest days in postwar Czech history. That night, military forces from the Soviet Union and several other Soviet-bloc nations invaded Czechoslovakia.

But the Czechs' desire for freedom outstripped the pace of these reforms. For many Czechs, particularly writers, artists, and intellectuals, the liberalization that took place in what came to be known as Prague Spring represented an opportunity to break free from the KPC altogether. Ludvik Vaculik, the editor of a popular literary journal, published a statement entitled, "Two Thousand Words to Workers, Farmers, Scientists, Artists and Everyone." The message of this document was clear: the recent reforms initiated by Dubcek and Svoboda from within the KPC were a start, but they did not go far enough. "After the war," Vaculik wrote, the party "possessed the great trust of the people." But it "gradually exchanged this trust for offices, until it had all offices and nothing else," and the party became "a power organization that became very attractive to egotists avid for rule, calculating cowards, and unprincipled people." He called for a complete end to the KPC's control over Czech society. The statement was discussed and signed by thousands of Czechs.

Dubcek and the liberal leaders within the KPC found themselves caught in the middle between this mass movement for increased freedoms and the Communist leaders, in Moscow as well as in Prague, who viewed the movement as a serious threat to their power. Leonid Brezhnev, leader of the Soviet Union, was demanding that Dubcek act against Vaculik and halt the reform program.

Dubcek steadfastly refused, and on the night of August 20, 200,000 soldiers moved into Czechoslovakia from 18 different invasion points. By the end of August, 650,000 troops occupied Czechoslovakia. In a matter of days, the democratic movement was crushed and its leaders— writers, artists, teachers—were removed from their professional posi tions and either jailed or made to work at menial jobs, as street sweepers and coal stokers and the like.

Martina and Vera ran to the window to get a glimpse of the Soviet tanks, but the house was on a side street and they were unable to see much. The tournament was canceled. Instead, the two girls remained indoors, playing cards and fuming at the Russians for ruining their play. In the evening, Mirek came on his motorcycle to Pilsen to retrieve Martina.

Resentment of the Soviet invasion was widespread and intense. While the Czech army had been ordered not to resist the invasion, ordinary Czech citizens used the weapons and tactics of the weak and unarmed: they threw rocks and rotten apples at the tanks; they refused to answer questions or give the Russian soldiers information or purposely misdirected them; they hung disdainful and taunting banners from the windows of their apartments; and they told anti-Communist jokes, like the one about Czechoslovakia having the biggest car in the world: "The seat is in Prague but the steering wheel is in Moscow." Martina claims to have thrown a few rotten apples herself.

Martina's parents were more interested in family life, sports, and the outdoors than they were in politics. Martina says that she does not know whether they signed the "Two Thousand Words." They were fortunate to be living in Revnice, in the countryside, where they did not have to wake in the morning with Russian soldiers on the streets outside their door, as did the residents of Prague.

Nevertheless, Martina's life changed greatly after the Soviet invasion brought a brutal end to Prague Spring. Her coach, George Parma, was among the 120,000 Czechs who defected after the invasion. From exile in the United States, he mailed outlines for his star pupil's tennis lessons, and Mirek became Martina's coach by proxy. Whenever Martina went to Prague, the sense of *litost* among the people would overwhelm her. There was less money available and little incentive for people to take pride in their work. Even at entertainment events like the opera or ballet, Martina could see that her fellow Czechs were dispirited, merely going through the motions of living a normal life. She was furious at the KPC bureaucrats who had stood by passively as the Soviet leaders drained the pride out of her country and turned its people into passive, sullen robots.

Martina sought refuge from her dismal surroundings by focusing completely on her tennis. Sports, especially tennis, were among the few inspiring—and politically safe—activities left in Czechoslovakia. Even so, the Czech Tennis Federation was controlled by KPC officials, who approached sports in the same regimented fashion they directed everything else: with a system of rules, incentives, and reinforcements.

Each time Martina won a tournament, she was given more court time to practice. And of course, each time she won, she became more personally invested in the game. The intention of the Czech Tennis Federation was to fuse a player's personal aspirations with the government's aspirations for them, so as to ensure that when Czech players began to compete on the international circuit, they would remain loyal to the government that had supported their development. It was also expected that any prize money an individual won was to be turned over to the Czech Tennis Federation, which would use it for facilities, equipment, and lessons for the next generation. All rising young athletes were encouraged, of course, to join the KPC.

Even people who were generally critical of the Communist regime marveled at this system's ability to produce disciplined, top-notch young athletes. But when it came to Martina, the system backfired. Or, more accurately put, Martina fired back at the system.

Martina grew up feeling violated by the government. She knew that when Czechoslovakia was an independent country, her family had owned an estate, and all the apple orchards she saw outside her window had belonged to them. At the same time, her family—perhaps with the exception of her grandfather—did not wallow in grief over their loss. Their enthusiasm for sports and their encouragement of Martina's athleticism instilled a kinesthetic sense of freedom in her that she would crave and cherish forever. By nature, Martina was also intellectually and physically more capable and more willful than most kids. The result of the combination of these factors was a young woman who just would not be collectivized.

As Martina grew, her sense of herself as an exceptional individual intensified. She experienced her athletic ability as her own: it did not belong to a country, or a government, or a tennis federation. Even as pressures to conform to the system and join the KPC mounted, Martina resisted. She used the pressure as a negative—"I'll show them"—incentive in her training and performance. Ultimately, Martina was prepared to risk her future options—for a college education and a tennis career—on her belief that skill, not obedience, would enable her to escape the system altogether.

Martina was permitted to leave Czechoslovakia for the first time in 1969. Her tennis club in Prague had an exchange program with a tennis club in West Germany, and with the Czech Tennis Federation's help, Martina and Mirek were able to secure visas and money to pay for a visit. The trip was Martina's first exposure to the comforts and riches of a Western, capitalist nation. West Germany was not as wealthy as the United States, but to Martina it was still pretty impressive. She was dazzled by the cars, the various food items, and the electric gadgets she saw: in Czechoslovakia, these items were luxuries that most did not have.

The youngest player in the tournament, Martina, in her own words, "beat the West German women players like a drum." She received a great deal of attention in the West German press and brought back the newspaper clippings as well as several medals to Czechoslovakia. It was clear to both Martina and to Czech tennis officials that she had great potential. The next year, when she won her first national title in the 14-and-under division, her victory made headlines throughout Czechoslovakia. Czech tennis fans began talking about the left-hander from Revnice as a star of the future. Every junior player in the country was out to beat her.

Martina began to get more time on the courts, particularly indoors. When she turned 15 she was invited by the federation to play at Sparta in Prague, one of the most famous sports clubs in Czechoslovakia. She played singles and was also placed on a team. Martina loved the camaraderie of the "family" of sports kids at Sparta: "When we weren't practicing, we'd hang around the clubhouse, playing chess and cards and just joking around."

In her autobiography, Martina described her new regimen as a "Sparta kid":

> To be able to use the Sparta facilities I had to rearrange my school schedule. The first year I went to school in Radotin, about halfway between Revnice and Prague. I'd take the 7:15 train in the morning, get to school at 7:45, then run for the 2:00 p.m. train to Prague.
>
> When I got off the train, I'd catch a tram, then change to another tram and then walk two miles up the hill to Sparta. I'd practice from 3:00 to

Czech belief in the importance of athletics predated the Communist era. Seen here are participants and observers at the quinquennial National Congress of Sokol (Falcon), a Czech gymnastic and patriotic society that was founded in 1862. Although the Communists repressed Sokol, they sought to channel the Czech tradition of mass participation in athletic activity into the kind of collective approach to sports training utilized by the Czech Tennis Federation.

5:00, then hustle to catch the 6:15 express train back to Revnice. If I missed that, I'd take the 6:40 local back. I'd be carrying all my gear and my books, same as always. I had no lockers either at school or at the tennis court, and there was homework every night. I'd prop my head on my two hands and hit the books until 10:30.

On the weekend, there were matches against other clubs—as many as 17 matches in a two-day meet, including singles, doubles, and mixed doubles. And there were trips to tournaments in other countries in Europe, to the Soviet Union and back to West Germany. For Martina, the schedule was grueling but invigorating.

In 1973 all the hard work and practice finally paid off. Martina was just 16 when she went after her first "adult" title, the Czech National Championship. During the early rounds, she beat many women who had been playing the game for years. In the semifinals, she was matched against the top player in her own Sparta Club, Renata Tomanova. Her victory over Tomanova set up a contest with Vlasta Vopickova, the number-one female player in the entire country. Despite a bad cold and a scraped knee, Martina won the final match, 7–5, 6–4. In both 1974 and 1975, she won again.

As an athlete, Martina had made the big time. But what about the rest of her life: school, friends, and the preoccupations of a "normal" teenager?

Although Communist countries encouraged all females to be active, a female professional athlete was still a rarity. There were few role models for such girls. Nor was Martina unaffected by images of glamorous women—movie actresses, the girlfriends and wives of tennis stars she met at tournaments—who exhibited the features of womanhood that were considered desirable in the West. At 14, Martina was especially concerned about the slow rate at which she was developing physically. She still had the sticklike figure of a young boy, narrow hips, nonexistent breasts, and no hair under her arms, and she had not started menstruating. Mirek tried to reassure her that she was developing normally and that she would get better-looking as she grew up. But when your peers are filling out and you are not, it is natural to worry and check your body every day for the signs of puberty.

At the same time, there was little room in Martina's life for indulging teenage anxieties or comparing notes with peers. Her physique did not prevent her from achieving what she and those around her—Mirek, her coach at Sparta, and her competitors—said was most important: training, playing, and winning at tennis.

In a restrictive world, Martina tried to maintain as much of a normal life as she could. It helped that her energy level was nearly limitless and that she had an outgoing and affable personality. Despite a demanding schedule of practice and travel on the international circuit, she continued to attend high school. She remained close friends with Kveta

Vlaskova, and they spent time together whenever Martina was in Revnice. She dated occasionally, and when she was 17, she became involved with a young man who was studying architecture at the university in Prague.

By this time, Martina had finally filled out, and her figure had some curves instead of resembling a stick with ears and feet. At first, she and her new friend's relationship was mostly platonic. They spent their time together playing tennis, going to the movies, walking through Prague, eating sausages and drinking beer, window-shopping, and looking for bars with American music. Martina felt comfortable with him and enjoyed his company. One evening after a date, he invited her to spend the night with him at his apartment.

Mirek, not Martina's mother, had been the one who told her about the facts of life. Like most parents in most countries, Mired communicated ambiguous rules and unclear messages to his daughter. He said it was not a good idea to have sex with someone unless you were married; or unless you were going to marry; or unless you were 21; or unless you were living together to test your compatibility before marriage. Like most teenage girls, Martina did not bother to unscramble all the "unlesses" and proceeded to engage in her first sexual adventure.

Physically, according to Martina, sex with her boyfriend was uncomfortable. There was also little emotional or physical desire; she was aware that she was not "in love" with him, that she loved him more like a brother. Although the two continued to see each other sporadically, the relationship was no rival for the attention and reinforcement that she received from playing professional tennis on the international circuit. And nothing in Czechoslovakia could compete with the love affair she was about to have—with America.

CHAPTER THREE

LEAVING HOME

For people who lived in the Soviet satellite countries of Eastern Europe, the United States epitomized the lavish lifestyle possible under Western capitalism. Eastern Europeans constructed their images of the United States mainly from two amusingly divergent sources: the analysis put forth by KPC officials in schools and newpapers about the gross economic and racial inequalities of capitalism and popular Hollywood movies of the 1950s and 1960s—dubbed in their native language and shown in local cinemas—that idealized and dressed up life in America.

In different ways, each source was a form of propaganda. The people of Eastern Europe knew all too well that Communists were capable of lying. However, Hollywood movies were not made by the government. These films came as a welcome treat and escape from the cold, drab, leveled society in which they lived. It was easy for the people to believe that they represented more of the "truth" about life in America than did the information they received from the Communist party.

The teenage Martina Navratilova who first set foot on American tennis courts in the early 1970s presented a far different figure from the superbly conditioned athlete who would dominate women's tennis in the next decade.

Like her compatriots, Martina spent many an afternoon sitting in the small, dark movie theater in Revnice, gaping at the cowboys and Indians in Hollywood Westerns and Fred Astaire, Ginger Rogers, Spencer Tracy, and Katharine Hepburn in frothy romantic comedies. Like most kids, she identified with the "good guys" and the "winners." As a child, Martina related in her autobiography, she often fancied herself a cowboy, climbing trees, brandishing a wooden pistol, and squaring off with the enemy. She also identified with the androgynous, sophisticated, sharp-edged persona of Hepburn.

However, as a professional athlete playing on the international tennis circuit, Martina was also exposed to images and sources of information about America to which her compatriots did not have access. Martina took special notice of black male athletes, whose apparent stature and success flew in the face of Communist criticism of racism in capitalist America. Their prominence reinforced her convictions about the importance of individual talent in overriding any political system. She also recognized that compared to Czechoslovakia's, the exchange rate for achievement and success in America was a lot higher.

In the dead of the snowy Czechoslovakian winter of 1973, Martina boarded an airplane in Prague and 18 hours later landed in Miami Beach, Florida. Accompanied by her doubles partner, Marie Neumannova, who was 10 years her senior and had been anointed by the Czech Tennis Federation to be her chaperone, Martina had been granted permission to play eight tournaments on the United States Tennis Association (USTA) tour. The excitement Martina had felt on earlier trips to the dazzling countries of Western Europe was merely a warm-up for the exhilaration she felt on arrival in the Sunshine State.

Wide-eyed, Martina took in the beaches; the bright pastel colors of the houses and motels; the sleek, huge American cars zooming along the interstates; and the friendly, talkative American people. She kept her mouth wide open too. The variety and quantity of food available at convenience stores and fast-food restaurants was simply too much temptation for this 16-year-old Czech kid with a little spending money—$11 dollars a day—in her pocket. For the entire six weeks she was in the States, Martina feasted on junk food and ice cream, which added a quick 20 pounds to her figure and quelled all her concerns about "filling out."

The vision of the young Martina, joyously bingeing on fast-food hamburgers, as if she might not ever get back to the States and had to fatten up for a lifetime of lean winters in Czechoslovakia, stood in stark contrast to the image of the American and Western European female players on the USTA tour, most of whom were obsessed with dieting and trying to look like the *prut* Martina had once been. Perhaps the contrast was starkest between Martina and the slender, blond, all-American tennis prodigy, Chris Evert. Evert, who normally weighed in at 120 pounds, was known to have begged reporters to write that her weight was "118."

In *Long Way, Baby*, her book about the 1973 USTA tour, Grace Lichtenstein took notice of the promising young foreign newcomer. She describes Martina as "a Czech left-hander, whose large, square build, high Slavic cheekbones and boyish manner suggested she would look just as at home in a Prague shoe factory as on a tennis court." About two weeks and 10 pounds into the tour, recounts Lichtenstein, Martina was sitting in the players' lounge in Philadelphia, munching a hamburger and giggling to others in her heavily accented English, "I cahn't beeleef I ate da whole t'ing," while pointing to her T-shirt, which was emblazoned with the same comic lament.

Both the American and the Russian players on the tour reacted to Martina's indulgence of her ravenous appetite with visible consternation. The Americans were taken aback because she was acting out their own worst nightmares of undoing years of controlled dieting and "pigging out" on everything in sight. The Russians worried that Martina was making a visceral and irreversible attachment to capitalism—through her stomach. Both were merciless in their ridicule of her appetite. The Americans referred to her as the "pancake champ" of the tour, and the Russians, Martina remembers, would pass her by, not saying a word, and just puff out their cheeks.

But perhaps for the first time in her life, Martina was exactly where she wanted to be, in America, playing with the legendary pros—including Evert, Billie Jean King, Virginia Wade, Evonne Goolagong, and

Margaret Court, the player whom Martina patterned herself after most—snacking her way across the country and drinking in the sights. Having studied English for only one semester in high school, she could not yet comprehend the subtleties of sarcasm and ridicule. Besides, in her world of comparisons, control and starvation had negative connotations. Actually, she thought she was looking pretty good, and healthy, and more feminine, and she was truly perplexed by the reaction of her peers. "What's their problem?" she wondered.

As it turned out, the Russians' concerns about Martina's attachment to America were warranted. Despite her weight gain, Martina performed well on the USTA tour, and the Czech Tennis Federation gave her permission to play in the French Open, one of the four most important tournaments in the world. (Together, Wimbledon, the U.S. Open, the French Open, and the Australian Open constitute the so-called grand slam of tennis.) There she defeated Nancy Richey—the United States's second-toughest red clay court player, right behind Chris Evert—6–3, 6–3, and made it to the quarterfinals before losing.

In the summer of 1974, Martina was allowed to play on another USTA tour. This time, she formed an irrevocable attachment to the people, the lifestyle, and the personal freedom she found in the United States.

The tour began in California. There Martina reconnected with her former coach, George Parma. As the tour wound its way east, she met other Czech exiles in Chicago, including Mirek and Svatka Hoschl, and Aja Zanova, the former world champion figure skater who had moved to New York City shortly after the Communist coup in 1951. Although they did not speak about politics directly, romanticize their life in America, or give Martina explicit ideas about leaving Czechoslovakia, these contacts acquainted Martina with the Czech community in the United States and provided her with attractive examples of what life could be like for a Czech exile. The Hoschls became part of Martina's extended family in the United States, and she could count on getting fed a traditional Czech dinner of duck and dumplings whenever she was in Chicago.

However, forming ties to the Czech community was not Martina's first priority. The most important thing was to figure out a way to become less bridled by the constraints imposed on her career and her finances by the Czech Tennis Federation. On the 1974 tour, Martina earned $3,000 in prize money, which she was expected to turn over to the federation when she returned to Prague. From the federation's point of view, Martina, as a professional athlete, was part of their national "capital," in whom they had made an investment. They had supported her training, provided facilities where she could practice, given her travel expenses, and even permitted her to keep a small percentage of her earnings. But as Martina saw it, her talent was hers alone, and therefore the money she won—all of it—should be hers as well. Her resentment of this financial arrangement came to a complete boil when federation officials instructed her to bring the prize money back in cash. Martina knew that in Czechoslovakia, American currency was useful only on the black market. This was corruption, not socialism.

It soon occurred to Martina that if the federation bureaucrats could wheel and deal, so could she. While playing in the 1974 U.S. Open in New York City, Martina was introduced to Fred Barman, the father of Shari Barman, one of the other players on the circuit. Barman, a movie agent in Los Angeles, was interested in building women's tennis into an entertainment industry. He offered to try to negotiate a financial deal between Martina and the federation.

Czech officials had little experience with Hollywood agents, and their first meeting with Barman was something of a shock. "The Czech Federation couldn't quite figure out who—or what—Fred was," Martina wrote in her autobiography. Nevertheless, a deal was struck. "The Czech Federation adjusted my earnings to an eighty-twenty split in my favor and, as Fred Barman likes to point out, the twenty percent I paid to the Federation was 'net, net, net.'" From Martina's share, the Internal Revenue Service would get nearly 30 percent in taxes.

With this extra money in her pocket, and an uncanny ability to befriend people despite language differences, Martina drifted away from the Czech and Eastern European players. She wanted to travel on the tour the way the American players traveled: staying in first-class hotels,

Among the attractions the United States held for Navratilova was the greater freedom she believed gay men and lesbians were afforded there. This photograph of gay activists was taken at the Christopher Street Liberation Day Parade in New York City in 1971.

hiring cars to chauffeur them from the hotel to the courts, and sending their laundry "out." She wanted all the opportunities and luxuries that Chris Evert had. The arrangement Barman negotiated was a first step toward achieving these things.

Finally, something else happened to Martina on this trip to the United States. Just as the American way of life helped make clear to Martina just what it was she wanted from her career, the more permissive social atmosphere of the United States brought about another kind of awareness about herself: that she was attracted to women. In Czechoslovakia, as in all Communist countries in this period, homosexuality was viewed as a disease. There was no such thing as a "gay" person. Indeed, an attempt to claim such an identity for oneself would make a citizen a "nonperson" in society. He or she might lose their job and, more likely than not, be confined to an institution for the mentally ill.

While some people would argue that the lot of gay people was not all that much better in America, where many states still maintained laws against "sodomy" and sexual preference was not included in most antidiscrimination policies, homosexuals were able to find acceptance as a "minority" in some social circles—primarily among artists, writers, and intellectuals. Moreover, a gay liberation movement did exist and was making some inroads into altering people's consciousness regarding homosexuality. Activists in the movement encouraged gay people to "come out of the closet" and be open about their homosexuality. Other social movements, most notably the women's movement, supported gay activism. Gay rights organizations, gay bookstores, and gay bars were established in most major urban centers around the country. By 1974 a visible though still quite marginal lifestyle—a way to be gay—had taken shape.

All this is not to suggest that Martina was immediately exposed to or even aware of this movement. Politically and culturally, the world of the gay liberation movement was quite removed from the world of the United States Tennis Association. Indeed, the world of professional sports tends to be conservative and "straight" in their attitudes about almost everything. In 1974, this world was not about to tolerate an openly gay figure in its midst, but as in most mainstream institutions, people looked the other way when same-sex relationships developed. Martina learned that there were gay people everywhere. With a little discretion and inventiveness, she could explore this emergent part of her identity.

The summer of 1974 had been an exciting period for Martina, a time when it became clear that she had the potential to be not just a world-class player but a dominating force in women's tennis. In a *Sports Illustrated* article that focused on the Virgina Slims tour, Martina was described as "the strongest woman in tennis, stronger even than [Margaret] Court." The prize money she was able to keep had been enough to buy her family their first car. She had transcended the boundaries—of language, reserve, and custom—that surrounded foreign players on the circuit and had made lots of acquaintances among the Americans.

It was not surprising, then, that when Martina returned to Czechoslovakia, she was restless and unhappy. Some of her complaints could be chalked up to the common miseries of adolescence. She was losing interest in her schoolwork and finding it difficult to readjust to living at home under parental supervision after being on her own for so many weeks. She missed her new friends in America. But unlike most 18-year-olds, who do not even know what they want to be when they grow up, Martina was already a "pro" and completely devoted to her career. If she remained in Czechoslovakia, that career would continue to be subject to control by the Czech Tennis Federation. They would determine where and when she would play, how she traveled, with whom she associated. These decisions would be made based on criteria—collective needs, party loyalty, political necessities—that might or might not coincide with her own needs and desires.

Still, Czechoslovakia was Martina's home, and her conflicting feelings made the fall of 1974 a very confusing time, as she explained in her autobiography: "I wandered about Revnice in a trance, playing with my puppy, Babeta. I visited friends, saw my boyfriend, spent time with Grandmother Subertova and took some long walks in the mountains above our town, gazing at the river and houses and asking myself: Are you really ready to say good-bye to this?"

Martina did not feel emotionally ready to make a decision that would change the course of her entire life. Defecting from Czechoslovakia would mean that there was a good chance that she would never see her family or her country again. She would not finish her high-school education. In the eyes of the Czech government, she would be an

In her early days on the women's professional tour, Navratilova's talent was obvious, but she required a greater sense of self-discipline to fulfill her potential.

outlaw, a nonperson. It also meant risking her family's security, her parents' jobs, and her sister Jana's options for education. Nor did Martina have a very clear idea of what life in America would hold for her. She felt confident in her ability to compete with the best tennis players in the world, and that, finally, was what mattered to her most. But every other aspect of her existence was a big question mark. Would she be granted political asylum by the United States and then citizenship? Where would she live? Who would be her "family?" What if she got hurt and was unable to play (her biggest fear of all)? The uncertainties were innumerable.

As Martina tells it, her personal inclination was to postpone this decision, maybe forever: to try to work out some arrangement with the Czech Tennis Federation whereby she would be given the freedom to pursue her tennis, to become an international star on the women's circuit, and still remain a Czech citizen. But as Martina sought an ever-greater degree of freedom—requesting permission to travel, adopting American styles in her appearance, hanging out with American players while on tour—the reins on her were pulled ever tighter.

Martina enjoyed the sympathy of some members of the Czech Tennis Federation. Her partner in mixed doubles, Jan Kodes, the women's coach, Vera Sukova, even the president of the federation, Antonin Himl, understood her aspirations. Nevertheless, they advised her to "cool it," to go along with the program in order to avoid trouble from high-level officials, in the federation and in the government, who strongly disapproved of her attitude and regarded her as a "nafoukana"—a young woman with her nose in the air, who viewed herself as exceptional and deserving of individual glory and compensation and was thereby a real threat to the Communist Ministry of Sport and a bad example for Communist youth.

The showdown came the following year, when the federation threatened to deny her permission to go to the United States and play in the 1975 U.S. Open. Martina mobilized her supporters, and the federation finally caved in and allowed her to go. However, the anticipation of a constant future struggle with the bureaucrats over each tournament, her training, her attitude, her money, and her accommodations and friends on tour was becoming unbearable. In the end, says Martina, "the bureaucrats made my decision to leave for me."

In her autobiography, she described the night before she left to play in the U.S. Open. She and Mirek went for a walk on the road near the river. Both Mirek and her mother knew how unhappy she was about how the federation was treating her. Personally, they had no special loyalty to the government and were proud that their daughter was independent enough, in a manner of speaking, to not allow the tanks to roll over her. Mirek told her that if she wanted to defect she should just stay in New York after the U.S. Open and do it. He said that she had the right to do whatever made her happy.

Even with Mirek's blessing, Martina could not quite admit to herself that this was really it. "I was ninety-five percent sure I was not coming back," she recalled in her autobiography. To be 100 percent sure, to have admitted that the decision had been made, would have meant having to say some very painful good-byes: to her mother, to Grandmother Subertova, and to her little sister. It might also have meant giving herself up to guilt feelings about abandoning her country and her family—no matter how legitimate her reasons were. Martina was not prepared to deal with all these emotions—few teenagers are. Besides, she had been well trained, as are all sports competitors, to be action-oriented, to tune out negative emotions, eliminate doubt, avoid conflict, focus on a goal, and keep her eye on the ball—just do it.

That same evening, Martina packed her clothes and fussed around the house. Her mother followed her around the flat, rubbing her hands together and smoking cigarettes. Although nothing was said, it was likely that Jana sensed that this might be the last time she would ever see her daughter. No one slept well that night, and in the morning Martina left for the airport.

CHAPTER FOUR

TRANSFORMATIONS

As she relates in her autobiography, Martina called Fred Barman as soon as she arrived in the States. As a friend and a kind of quasi-manager, Barman was the closest thing to an adult caretaker that Martina had in the United States. She asked him to hire a lawyer who could arrange for her to apply for asylum in the United States. Such arrangements had to be made very discreetly, since there was a real risk that if Czech officials found out about Martina's plan they could stop it, either by putting pressure on the U.S. government to refuse her asylum or, less likely, by abducting her back to Czechoslovakia.

Despite the tension, Martina performed well in the U.S. Open, making it to the semifinals, where even while losing in straight sets to Chris Evert she put up a good fight. That evening, Friday, September 5, she was accompanied by Barman, an attorney, and two F.B.I. agents to the Manhattan office of the Immigration and Naturalization Service, where she formally requested that the United States grant her political asylum. By the time she returned to her hotel, the

Navratilova makes the "V for victory" sign as she meets the press on September 7, 1975, to announce that she had received political asylum in the United States. "It was my decision alone," she said. "I did it to further my tennis career."

sensational story had already been leaked to the press, and she was forced to hide out from the besieging horde of reporters at the apartment of Jeanie Brinkman, publicity director for the Virginia Slims tour.

On Sunday morning, Martina returned to Forest Hills, site of the U.S. Open, where she held a press conference right before the men's final. Her hands shook and she laughed nervously as the journalists fired questions at her. They pressed her to admit, as the Czech Tennis Federation had maintained in its official statement, that money was the main motivation for her defection. "Navratilova had all the possibilities in Czechoslovakia to develop her talent, but she preferred a professional career and a fat bank account," stated the federation, which noted that she had already made $140,000 in 1975 and went on to add that in the United States she would not be made to finish her education.

The money was one factor, Martina tried to explain, but not simply the only or decisive one. She mentioned the freedom to control her own career in all its aspects. The mention of "freedom" inspired questions about political ideology and comparisons between communism and capitalism, with Martina attempting to communicate that she was not leaving Czechoslovakia for overtly political reasons. The following day, the story appeared on the front page of the *Washington Post*.

But Martina's nervousness, her inability to communicate as well as she might have wished in English, and the desire of reporters to put an appealing slant on the story resulted in a different interpretation in some organs of the press. Under pressure, at her press conference Martina had called "crazy" those Americans who criticized their society. "Any American who complains about this country should go to Europe or anywhere else in the world for two years. You don't know what you've got here," she said. Such comments were seized upon by American political conservatives, who were eager to make Martina a prominent symbol of the repressiveness of the Communist system. In conservative areas of the country, she became something of a fan favorite because of this image of her as an anti-Communist. However, in the months that followed, when she was given time to reflect and speak more measuredly, Martina refuted this characterization of her as a political dissident. "Communism is a good system," she said, "if it is run by the right people. It has faults, but there are faults in every system."

Martina had one more motive for leaving—one that she was not about to reveal to the press. It would be quite some time, nearly 20 years in fact, until Martina would see a good reason to provide the missing piece in the puzzle of her defection. "I left Czechoslovakia about three months after I realized I was gay," she said in 1993 in an interview with the *Advocate,* a national gay and lesbian magazine. "I knew I couldn't be gay in Czechoslovakia." But as she saw it in 1975, her sexuality was no one's business but her own.

Martina's application for asylum was processed routinely. U.S. immigration policy generally sanctioned the granting of political asylum to individuals who managed to leave a country in the Communist bloc. Indeed, Martina had been the fourth internationally known athlete to defect from Czechoslovakia since 1948. On October 6, 1975, her application for asylum was approved. She received her green card, a document that allowed her to live and work legally in the United States. In five years' time, she could apply for full citizenship. In the midst of a transformation of its own, the U.S. women's tennis tour— more successful, better publicized, more competitive, and more lucrative than ever—eagerly awaited her arrival as a full-time player.

At the same time that Martina was fighting the Czech Tennis Federation, women players in the United States were waging a rebellion of their own against the official governing body of tennis in America, the United States Lawn Tennis Association (USLTA; now the United States Tennis Association, or USTA). The grievances of the American women focused on the elitist and sexist stereotypes according to which the game had been governed since its inception, traditions of inequality that had prohibited women from competing professionally and earning a living at the sport.

These traditions dated back to the late 19th century, when tennis was introduced in the United States as a recreational pastime for the wealthy—those with an abundance of leisure time and enough personal property on which to build courts. Shortly thereafter, upper-class tennis enthusiasts formed the USLTA, investing it with the power to organize tournaments, conserve traditions of on-court behavior, dress, and etiquette, and establish and enforce the rules of the game.

At the time, tennis was considered less a sport, with connotations of vigorous physical exertion, unbridled competition, unchecked masculinity, and democratic participation, especially by members of the lower classes, than it was a form of "recreation," refined, tame, and proper enough to permit the participation of women. Women played tennis under the same physical and social restrictions that regulated their appearance and behavior off the court. They wore skirts that reached to the ground with several layers of petticoats underneath; their shirts featured long sleeves, buttons to the neck, and stiff high collars; and large floppy hats shielded their faces from the sun's glare. They were not expected to run for the ball or hit it hard. Their decorum during the game reflected all the manners considered appropriate for upper-class ladies of the Victorian era.

Tennis grew steadily in popularity throughout the 20th century. Courts were built in recreational clubs, public parks, and even on the grounds of public high schools, providing new, less-privileged players with access to the game. The expansion of the game into the public sphere also attracted spectators and tennis fans—those who enjoyed the vicarious excitement of watching the game and cheering on the players.

The new players—those who emerged from the public courts and the less affluent clubs—posed a serious threat to the traditions of tennis. They did not have time to play the game purely for recreation; they could not afford membership in posh, private tennis clubs where tournaments were held; and they had little investment in maintaining standards of etiquette that impeded their ability to compete.

The USLTA viewed this challenge to tradition as a degradation of the game. For many years, they resisted making tennis into a purely professional sport by making secret payments "under the table" to popular but less affluent players. In the 1960s, however, a time of social upheaval when many American institutions were compelled to remove the economic, racial, and sexual barriers that restricted opportunities for underrepresented segments of the population, the USLTA succumbed to pressure. It opened competition in the game and sanctioned a limited number of "professionals." These individuals played tennis on a full-time basis, receiving subsidies for travel and lodging and "bonuses" for winning matches.

Billie Jean King, the daughter of a fireman from Long Beach, California, was the most prominent female player in this new generation of aspiring professionals. From 1966 on, she dominated competition on the women's tennis circuit and was vocal in expressing her impatience with the USLTA's resistance to reform. Inspired by her own working-class origins and the rise of feminism in the United States, King became an advocate of professionalism as well as women's equality in tennis.

In the early 1970s, King helped found several women's professional organizations—including the Virginia Slims circuit, the Women's Tennis Association, World Team Tennis, and the Women's Sports Foundation—all of which challenged the USLTA's claim to be the sole authority running women's professional tennis. In 1972, she challenged the discrepancies in treatment and prize money that existed between the men and women on the open circuit.

King's efforts were successful, in part because of her tenacity as an organizer, in part because she had the support of most of her peers, and

Billie Jean King (left, with the winner's trophy at Wimbledon in 1968) had long been an inspiration to Navratilova, who said in 1975 that she had wanted to be the best women's tennis player in the world "ever since I was nine years old when I saw Billie Jean King winning Wimbledon on television."

in part because her vision received financial backing from large corporations, including Philip Morris, Avon Cosmetics, and Kraft Foods. The chief executives of these companies believed that the "liberation" of women's professional tennis had tremendous commercial value. If packaged correctly, both the game and the accoutrements of the young female players—their rackets, sneakers, athletic bags, makeup, even the aspirin they took for their menstrual cramps—could be sold to the American consumer. The promotion of the new female tennis player as a model of fitness and femininity would also contribute to a host of other auxiliary enterprises, including health clubs, equipment, workout manuals, and paraphernalia that would allow ordinary women to feel like a pro. Big money was devoted to making women's professional tennis an entertainment and advertising spectacle. All sorts of middlemen—promoters, agents, managers, publicists—were involved in the endeavor. It became the first—and remains the only—women's sport to be televised on a regular basis.

This new order in women's tennis created a plethora of new opportunities for the top-ranked players. Other corporations followed the lead of Virginia Slims cigarettes and created women's tennis circuits of their own—both inside and outside the United States. Women received larger amounts of money for winning tournaments and in general benefited from many more ways to make money, including commercial endorsements and appearances at exhibition matches.

The new order had a downside, however, especially as regards the social lives and development of the players. In *Long Way Baby*, Grace Lichtenstein described women's tennis before it became a business. In the amateur days, the players traveled from tournament to tournament as a group. They shared rooms in cheap motels or stayed as guests in the homes of wealthy tennis club members, fans, or friends—a practice that was referred to as "staying with people." Although it was every woman for herself on the court, off court the women socialized with each other constantly—bantering in the locker room, eating meals together, sitting with one another and kibbitzing in the stands when they were not playing. "This was a unique congregation of women," wrote Lichtenstein, "a cross between a sorority and a summer camp, a team and a tribe, a jock sisterhood. I was moved by the genuine respect and affection they had for one another."

But as the number of tournaments and the available prize money grew and the diversity of sponsors and level of competition increased, women's tennis began to attract younger and younger players as professionals. At the age of 12 or 13, girls who showed promise were encouraged to turn pro. "The life" for these young girls was quite different from that of their predecessors. For eight months out of the year they traveled from tournament to tournament, neither alone nor together but with a private entourage that included family members, friends, managers, secretaries, coaches, hitting partners, and even a masseuse. Although each member of the entourage had an assigned role in catering to the needs of the player, they were unified in one ultimate purpose: to protect the young player and shut out any stimulus that did not directly contribute to her ability to compete.

In *Courting Fame: The Perilous Road to Women's Tennis Stardom*, author Karen Stabiner describes how drastically removed these girls are from anything resembling "normal" childhood or adolescence: "What might be considered healthy interests in another child come to be regarded as distractions for the gifted, ambitious player. Girls often give up attending school because it gets in the way of practice—at fifteen, their education consists of completing an assignment and stuffing it into a mailbox, to be sent to a correspondence school. They curtail their social life to fit around their sports schedule, or find it has been curtailed for them." Young players remain isolated from each other, cloistered in private hotel suites and ushered from place to place in private limousines. Even in the close quarters of the locker room, interaction among the players is rare: young girls wait their turn to play in the company of a family member or coach or while listening to music through a headset.

While the new order had clearly liberated these girls from certain conventions of femininity—in the areas of competition and money—it left other restraints intact. One of the ways in which girls are discouraged from getting involved in sports is through propagation of a two-sided myth: (1) women athletes are not "real" women, i.e., they are women who would really rather be men; and (2) involvement in athletics turns women into lesbians. Any promotion of female athleticism, it would seem, would at least by implication involve a challenge to this myth. Yet those involved in the transformation of women's tennis into a big business had no intention of meeting this challenge.

Promoters marketed their young female tennis "phenoms" in the unthreatening image of a starlet or, in Stabiner's words, "a pint-sized goddess"—sweet, innocent, toylike little girls whose outsized talent propels them into worldwide celebrity. To this end, sponsors sought out young, white, cute, middle-class, ostensibly heterosexual females to represent the game and become walking billboards for their equipment and clothing lines. Agents who made endorsement deals encouraged this image by distributing to corporate sponsors photographs of their clients dressed not as tennis players but as fashion models.

Women who did not conform to this Shirley Temple–like image—because of their looks, their size, their age, or their reputed lifestyle—were devalued, hidden, or if possible, "remade." This commercial enterprise created unreal expectations for all the women and girls, but the experience of lesbian women was especially damaging and contradictory. In the everyday reality of the women's circuit, lesbians and lesbian relationships were treated matter-of-factly. According to Billie Jean King in her book *We Have Come a Long Way,* "the gays and straights and bisexuals on tour co-exist wonderfully and it's no big deal." Mariah Burton Nelson, a former professional basketball player who has written several books on gender and sports, confirms that in the course of the day-to-day life of the tour, the fact that some women are gay is of no great interest to most players: "Once they have sorted out who's who, they choose friendships on the basis of other factors—a similar sense of humor, a mutual love of movies, shared political concerns." However, as the sport was presented in public—at press conferences, in advertisements, at exhibitions—the reality that some players were lesbians was completely denied.

At the time Martina arrived on the tour, women's tennis was in the throes of this transformation. The players from the old days, the

Navratilova serves at the U.S. Open in 1975. The scene of her public announcement of her defection from Czechoslovakia, the Open would also be the site of some of her greatest on-court disappointments.

pioneers of change—including Billie Jean King, Rosie Casals, and Evonne Goolagong—were still competing and were finally making some big money. In a very short time, women's professional tennis had come a long way, and these women were enjoying the fruits of their labor. At the same time, they seemed able to preserve some of the more sociable aspects of the women's circuit of the "old days."

Martina, however, was a part of a transitional generation of players. Her contemporaries were the younger Chris Evert, Andrea Jaeger, Tracy Austin, and Pam Shriver. For a time, this "second" generation had the opportunity to observe and participate in the sorority-like atmosphere that their predecessors had created. Perhaps more than any of her contemporaries, Martina loved the camaraderie among the women. It reminded her of life as a Sparta kid in Czechoslovakia and provided her with a sense of having a family. But as the older women retired, the sorority gradually disbanded. Increasingly, the careers and lives of Martina and her generation would be defined by requisites of the new order.

CHAPTER FIVE

THE PRINCESS
AND THE ALIEN

In many ways, Navratilova fit easily into the new world of professional tennis. She relished the competition and the opportunity to display her talent in front of thousands of spectators. Whereas some players felt that they were pushed to compete by aspiring parents and coaches, Navratilova was internally motivated. She genuinely loved the game, so much so that she had left behind her homeland and family for the freedom to play it the way she wanted to play it.

In the months following her defection, she won two championships in singles and two in doubles and was named the "most improved" player of 1975, although she still had not captured a title in a major tournament. Her serve was up to 91 miles an hour. *Tennis* magazine ranked her number four on the women's circuit, behind Billie Jean King, Chris Evert, and Evonne Goolagong. In addition, she was a great success in the newly formed World Team Tennis league as a member of the Cleveland Nets. The brainchild of promoters

Navratilova, the victor (left), receives a congratulatory embrace from the vanquished Chris Evert at Wimbledon in 1978. Though the press liked to portray the two on-court competitors as constant rivals, they are actually close friends.

and business agents, including Martina's manager, Fred Barman, team tennis was developed early in 1974. It was conceived as a way of increasing tennis's popularity as a spectator sport by appealing to Americans' love of team competition. Sixteen teams, based in major cities around the nation, were formed, each one featuring three men and three women competing as a team. Although World Team Tennis never attained a great deal of stability and some teams folded in the first year, the Cleveland Nets endured. Martina was cited as one of the most valuable players in the league and was reportedly paid $300,000 for her signature on a three-year contract. She never missed a contest while winning 227 matches against 198 losses.

Beyond the professional respect she earned as an emerging world-class player, Martina was well liked by the other players on the circuit. In *We Have Come a Long Way*, Billie Jean King remarks on the ease with which Martina mastered the English language; in a short time she was able to spice up conversations with jokes and slang phrases, making evident her intelligence and wit. Later on, Martina's contemporaries would make similar observations, noting that even under the cutthroat pressures of the new order, she remained a sociable and supportive peer.

However, as corporate interests became increasingly important in women's tennis, performing well on the court and being a decent person off the court were just not enough: to be the ultimate success, a player had to have the right look, the right clothes, the right hairdo, the right mannerisms, and the right lifestyle. It was this obsession with "image" that initially made Navratilova, whatever her achievements, a marginal and problematic figure in this world. Indeed, the tennis establishment had already selected a young woman to be the "poster girl" for the new generation of players long before Navratilova set foot in the United States. Chris Evert was the female player against whom all other players—and if sponsors had their way, all other females—would be measured.

In 1971, Evert, at the age of 16, had become the youngest pro on the open circuit. She had grown up in a conservative, middle-class Catholic family in Fort Lauderdale, Florida. She wore pinafore dresses and ribbons in her hair. She was slim and demure. She even played the sport like a lady, hitting even ground strokes from the baseline and seldom displaying emotion during her matches, keeping so cool that some dubbed her the "ice princess." At 18, she started dating her counterpart on the men's circuit, the handsome and dashing Jimmy Connors, and the two were presented as tennis's Cinderella and Prince Charming. For corporate America, "Chrissie" Evert could not have presented a more perfect image: a wholesome, ladylike child champion who, it seemed, rarely even broke a sweat on the court.

Navratilova, on the other hand, was a big, tough, overweight "foreigner." Her Czech origins were still audible in the accent with which she spoke English. Her approach to the sport was unapologetically athletic. Her arms and legs bulged with muscles. She played tennis aggressively, rushing the net and taking risks. Her demeanor was anything but ladylike. She expressed everything she was feeling, even during matches. She scowled. She laughed. She stamped her feet. She slapped her hand to her forehead. She yelped for joy. She argued. And she was completely on her own. There was no family to fawn over her, and there were no boyfriends in sight.

As it became increasingly clear that Navratilova was going to be Evert's top on-court challenger and that the two would be likely to contend against each other for the top singles titles for years to come, the tennis establishment had to figure out a way to market the show. They promoted the rivalry between Navratilova and Evert as a battle of opposites. Evert was cast as the favorite, the homegrown, all-American princess. Navratilova was the underdog, the intriguing but strange rough-around-the-edges alien, who had escaped from behind the Iron Curtain with only her tennis racket.

To their credit, Navratilova and Evert did not allow this contrived marketing representation to affect their personal interactions. In fact, the two became close friends. And when they teamed up as doubles partners, the opposites image was somewhat diluted. But there was no escaping the disparities in their experiences as players and as women. Evert had the right "image." During matches, she had the support of the crowd. After matches, she went on dates with her boyfriend.

For Navratilova, visits from family members were rare during the first years after her defection. In March 1979, her beloved grandmother Andela Subertova was on hand to watch her win the Virginia Slims championship at Madison Square Garden in New York City.

And when the season was over, she went home, to her family and friends.

Navratilova, meanwhile, was a girl on her own. She did what she could to combat her loneliness and insecurity. When not with the tour, she stayed at the Barmans' home in Los Angeles. She spoke with her parents on the phone almost every week. She looked forward to playing team tennis, where she was constantly surrounded by teammates. While on tour, she amused herself during off hours by watching soap operas on television, doing crossword puzzles, or reading mysteries.

Navratilova also pursued a few sexual adventures with women. Although none of them lasted for any significant length of time, she now felt certain about her sexual orientation. She knew after her first sexual experience with a woman that she was going to be gay for the rest of her life.

Less certain was how she was going to manage dating and relationships as a gay woman inside a world that was so closely monitored—by officials, sponsors, and the press—and in which image was everything. She did not like having to hide her personal life and believed—perhaps naively—that her achievements in tennis would outweigh any prejudice she might encounter. But the other players she knew who were gay kept it a secret, fearing that revealing the truth could have negative economic consequences. "I wouldn't want to buy a racquet if a homosexual plays with it," Gladys Heldman, publisher of *World Tennis* magazine, bluntly stated, and corporate sponsors feared that such sentiments were widespread.

Personally, Navratilova had a hard time understanding such sentiments, especially in a country that prided itself on the freedom of expression allowed its citizens. But there were no positive role models for her to follow. The gay women she knew had no sense of community or history as lesbians, and they kept their distance from gays who were "out" or who looked gay or too "dykey." Essentially, Navratilova was living in a world that, according to Mariah Burton Nelson, is "held hostage to fear of the 'L-word.'" So, like the rest, Navratilova learned to keep her guard up. Reluctantly and resentfully, she adhered to the requisites of life "in the closet." Eventually, her honesty and unwillingness to lie would separate her from her gay counterparts in the sports world, but for the present, a string of unsuccessful affairs, combined with the need for secrecy, contributed to a sense of despair that had been mounting since her defection.

For the most part, Navratilova dealt with her sadness by putting into zealous practice the modern American maxim, "when the going gets tough, the tough go shopping." In 1976, at the ripe old age of 20, she was already a wealthy woman. Between her earnings from tournaments, her contract for World Team Tennis, and endorsement deals for sneakers, socks, and tennis rackets, she was already approaching millionaire status. Whereas in 1973 she had consumed hamburgers on her spending allowance, she now consumed consumer items commensurate with the size of her pocketbook. She became a regular at Neiman Marcus and in the boutiques on Rodeo Drive in Beverly Hills. She bought a Mercedes sports car, Gucci handbags, and gold jewelry and gave generous gifts to others. She was even able to buy a new house for her parents and sister in Czechoslovakia. It was intoxicating for her to spend more money on just one dinner in a restaurant than her father earned in a year. Nor was she daunted by those who ridiculed her forays into the depths of American-style conspicuous consumption: she was known to appear on court wearing all—sometimes as many as eight bracelets, several necklaces, and diamond earrings—of what she had purchased on a recent spree.

Though she liked being rich, she still, try as she might, could not lull herself into happiness with toys and cars and jewelry. Her loneliness would not go away. Worse yet, her state of mind was beginning to affect her tennis, which remained inconsistent, more promise than performance. She was still overeating, still consuming too much junk food. At Wimbledon in 1976, the press ridiculed her for her weight and labeled her "the great wide hope" of women's tennis. She suffered some minor but nagging injuries to her wrist, not serious enough to sideline her but harmful enough to hamper her play. She was not practicing enough and was growing exhausted from all the travel demanded of her.

At the 1976 U.S. Open at Forest Hills, on the first anniversary of her defection, Navratilova came unhinged. "I got to Forest Hills," she recounted in her autobiography, "and all the memories of 1975 came flooding in on me. I kept having flashbacks of my trips to the Immigration Service, the fears of being kidnapped by Communist officials, the worries about where I would live. I had put a lid on my emotions surrounding my defection for a whole year, but as soon as I opened up the racquet bag at Forest Hills, they swarmed out like termites in the spring and they ate me alive."

She was scheduled to play her opening round in the tournament against the unheralded Janet Newberry, but rain delayed the match for several hours. Knowing that she was unprepared, both physically and psychologically, to play, Navratilova inquired about getting the match postponed, but her unusual request was denied, and when the rain let up, the two players took the court.

Losing is hard enough, but losing in the first round to an unseeded player is humiliating. When the match was over, Navratilova headed for a courtside bench and just sat there, sobbing and moaning. She threw a towel over her head to hide her tear-stained face from the cameras. With her head still covered, she then made her way to the locker room, where she stayed under the shower as long as possible. Fred Barman stood outside and ran interference with the sportswriters, who were eager to question her about the tantrum, which was something they would never have seen, for example, from the always properly composed Chris Evert. As soon as Navratilova returned to her hotel room, she pulled out of her doubles match, which was scheduled for the next day. After a year of pretending that her new life in America would just magically fall into place, Navratilova was thrown back in memory to that hillside in Revnice—the last place and time where she had allowed herself to think about all the uncertainties in her future. Nothing had been resolved.

Navratilova marks this outburst as the nadir of her career, but there would be other low points as well. Even the most outstanding professional lives do not follow a steady, constant path upward. Careers of achievement tend to spiral. Setbacks are inevitable. The sign of a champion is being able to mobilize new resources in periods of difficulty and crisis.

In her battle with the Czech Tennis Federation, Navratilova had demonstrated a tenacious capacity to turn obstacles into motivation. The "okay-the-world-is-against-me-but-I'll-show- them" attitude that she first exhibited at that time would serve her well in times of crisis. Because of the love and support that she had been given by her mother, stepfather, and grandmother, she knew how to ask for and accept help. She also seems to have had a knack for finding people who were willing to assist her. Generally, the people she turned to were somewhat older women who were perceived as wiser than herself.

On the day following Navratilova's loss at the U.S. Open, just such a woman arrived at the door of her hotel room. Navratilova had met Sandra Haynie, a professional golfer, a few months earlier and had invited her to New York to watch her play in the tournament. But by the time Haynie arrived, the U.S. Open, at least as far as Navratilova was concerned, was over. She confided her embarrassment and confusion about her future to this veteran professional athlete and new friend. Haynie comforted her by explaining the spiral theory of career development and offered to take her under her wing and help put her career back together.

With that, Navratilova said good-bye to the Barmans and to Los Angeles and moved to Dallas, Texas, to be with Haynie. The two bought a three-bedroom ranch house on the north side of town, complete with a swimming pool and jacuzzi, and wasted no time in setting out to design a training regimen that would get Navratilova into better condition.

Though Navratilova loved to play sports, she was not fond of exercise for exercise's sake. But the improved athleticism of the new players on the women's tour demanded a fitter, more versatile, and more health-conscious player. Under Haynie's tutelage, Navratilova came to realize that she could not feed her body hamburgers and Coke and pancakes drenched in sugary syrup, lounge at poolside or in front of the television in her downtime, and then just will her body to respond to the demands of the moment when it was time to play. If she was going to make it to the top in a sport that was constantly recruiting ever younger and more agile players, she would have to be more respectful of her body, to recognize that it had needs of its own for working out, resting, efficient fueling, and constant fine-tuning.

Navratilova and Haynie joined a fitness club, and they started jogging a few miles each day. Haynie encouraged Navratilova to practice for longer periods of time and to play in more tournaments. She also helped her to change her diet, by cooking healthful meals at home and eliminating junk food from the menu. But the major lesson she taught Navratilova was psychological, not physical: how to control her moods to prevent them from interfering with her concentration on the court.

Navratilova was an attentive student. Having a companion, a home, and a domestic life gave her a sense of well-being. She even started managing her money better and investing some of it, instead of spending it all. She dropped nearly 15 pounds and felt in control of herself, and her game picked up almost immediately.

When the 1978 season commenced, Navratilova exploded onto the circuit. She won 37 straight matches on the Virginia Slims circuit and won the French Open. Between tournaments she maintained her practice and fitness regimen, intent on winning Wimbledon, the most hallowed, revered tournament of them all.

Meeting her friend and toughest opponent, Chris Evert, in the finals at Wimbledon made Martina more than nervous. She lost the first set

Navratilova's mother helps her celebrate her singles championship at Wimbledon in 1979.

decisively, but in the first game of the next set something happened. "Chris hit a passing shot at an angle," Navratilova later recalled, "and the ball hit me right in the head. It didn't really hurt, it woke me up. I won the next two sets 6–4, 7–5 and fulfilled the dream of my—and my father's—lifetime." The alien had defeated the princess at Wimbledon, and for the first time Navratilova captured the biggest tennis title in the world.

True to form, she slapped her hand to her forehead in disbelief. She and Evert shook hands, and Evert put her arm around her. As the two friends and competitors waited for the Duchess of Kent to present the trophies, Evert asked jestingly, "How come you're not crying, Martina?"

"I am," she answered, "but I'm practicing how not to show it."

Four days later, the Women's Tennis Association's computerized rankings placed Navratilova number one in the world, breaking Evert's four-year domination of the top slot. "I felt I was on top of the world and that I'd stay there forever," she recalled in her autobiography.

She remained on top through the entire next year. Back at Wimbledon in 1979, she hoped to win the championship again, but this time the victory would be even sweeter. Someone very special would be watching her from the stands.

As a rule, Czech expatriates cannot return for a visit to their homeland until they become citizens of another country. Navratilova had applied for a waiver of this policy, but it had been denied. However, in 1979 the Czech government agreed to issue her mother a travel visa that would allow her to attend Wimbledon. As it was government policy to allow only one member of a family out of the country at a time to ensure their return, Mirek and her sister, Jana, had to stay behind.

It had been almost four years since mother and daughter had seen each other. In the hope of avoiding the press, Navratilova drove alone to the airport, where she watched her mother descend from the airplane carrying a box of fresh-baked cookies. The reunion, as one would expect, was very emotional, and Jana worried that all the emotion would detract from her daughter's ability to play.

As Navratilova defended her title, her mother sat quietly in the players' box, with her hands folded atop her pocketbook. She was very nervous and kept looking from side to side to make sure that she was applauding at the right times. When it was over, and Martina had once again taken the championship from Chris Evert, beating her 6–4, 6–4 in the finals, the cameras turned toward the stands, searching for Jana Navratilova. They zoomed in just in time to see this heretofore reserved woman jump up and dance around her seat with joy. Now the entire world could see that Martina was not so strange. She was definitely someone's daughter: Jana Navratilova's sudden outburst was ample proof that Martina came by her emotionality honestly.

Amid ringing applause, Navratilova walked onto Centre Court and curtsied to the royal box, where the Duchess of Kent sat beaming approval in the direction of a recomposed Jana Navratilova. Later, a reporter asked the mother if her daughter had changed since she last saw her in 1975. "Yes," she said in her best English. "I think she is very pretty now. Now she is skinnier."

The career slump of 1976 was history. Navratilova had achieved precisely what she had come to the United States to do: she was a world-class tennis professional, a Wimbledon champion, the number-one player in the USTA rankings. The spiral was heading upward. She felt confident about her ability to stay on top. Even her image was improving. It was now time to "smell the roses"—to explore some of life's pleasures beyond training and playing tennis.

While Haynie had been invaluable in helping Navratilova to mature, to take control of her mind and body, and to develop the mental strength that makes a champion athlete, their relationship was not entirely satisfying. Haynie preferred to live a quiet, disciplined existence all the time. "She was a good calming influence on me for a few years," Navratilova explains in her autobiography, "but I was trying to find the world outside and Haynie was happy sitting around watching TV. . . . not that I was much for night life either, but I wanted to get around a little more."

Navratilova felt increasingly restless and stifled by the routines of her domestic and professional life. She wanted something—or, someone— new, different, exciting. So she did what she already had some practice in doing: she packed up and left home. Once separated from Haynie, Martina had a brief relationship with an unnamed woman, apparently someone of considerable stature. But soon thereafter, she met someone who would become a major love and influence in her life.

That someone was Rita Mae Brown. Once again, Navratilova had chosen an older and wiser woman, but this woman's wisdom and passions had little to do with tennis and sports. By 1979, Brown had already written three novels, one of which was the best-seller *Rubyfruit Jungle*. Told in the voice of a bold, funny, slightly outrageous young girl who was not ashamed or frightened by any of the "perversions" human sexuality has to offer, *Rubyfruit Jungle* was the first upbeat coming-out story. It has become a classic in gay literature. If anyone could expose Navratilova to a broader political and cultural world, it would be this writer, activist, and supersophisticated, out-of-the-closet lesbian.

CHAPTER SIX

MARTINA
MEETS A FURY

Whether Brown pursued Navratilova or vice versa depends a great deal on who is doing the telling. In her autobiography, Navratilova explains that she was playing in a tournament in Virginia when she was told by a fellow player, Wendy Overton, that a writer friend was interested in meeting her, ostensibly for the purpose of doing research for the creation of a Czech character in her next novel. The idea did not particularly excite her. When she learned that the writer was Rita Mae Brown, whose *Rubyfruit Jungle* she had read, she was a "little more interested, but only a little." Nevertheless, "the first time we met," Navratilova wrote,

> I felt Rita Mae wanted to know everything about me. . . . What was the invasion like? What were the Communist teachers like? What about women's rights in Czechoslovakia? What did I feel about it all? I remember thinking, My God, nobody ever asked me these questions before. . . . It was exciting.

A quintet of stars from the Women's Tennis Association: standing (from left) are Rosie Casals, Billie Jean King, and Tracy Austin. Navratilova kneels next to Chris Evert. Navratilova loved the camaraderie of life on the women's circuit.

We shook hands and promised to keep in touch. I saw her briefly in Phoenix that fall and I didn't talk to her, at all. Then I ended up calling her after New Year's and we started talking on the phone almost every day, and then we finally met in Chicago.

Brown's recollections are somewhat different:

Martina came to my attention when she was 15, when she played a few tournaments in the U.S. Having been number one on my college team, I kept up with tennis and still had a few old friends on the tour. She was very fat and very talented, and I predicted to Steve Kinzer, then with the *Boston Globe,* that she would lose weight and have a great career.

Years later, a mutual friend got us together for lunch in Richmond, Virginia, where she was playing a tournament in August of 1978. I liked Martina and her then-girlfriend very much. In January, Martina and her friend were pulling apart and she started calling me. I'd written her letters, I love to write friends letters, so I had stayed in touch with both of them. She hasn't much patience with waiting, and I'm quite slow about these kind of things. She prevailed though, and I flew out to meet her in Chicago.

Even though she courts you like crazy, I mean it's absolutely obsessive, I still wouldn't say that she initiated the relationship. For all the speed, there was an organic quality to the union.

Even before meeting Brown, Navratilova's political outlook—had she been given an opportunity to articulate it—might have been labeled "feminist." In Communist Czechoslovakia, where equality for women was the official party line, Navratilova had been socialized to think that women were entitled to the same opportunities as men—in both love and work. Martina's mother was a good example of this "emancipated" woman—she was active in sports, she worked outside the home, she had been divorced and then remarried, and she encouraged her daughter to pursue her athletic interests without restraint.

However, Communist notions about women's emancipation were based on equality with men, not independence from men. The idea that women could have lives separate from men—socially or sexually—was not condoned in Communist societies. While Navratilova's primary motivation for leaving Czechoslovakia was to gain independence as a tennis player, she also sensed that her career was not the only thing in jeopardy, that as a lesbian, she was not going to fit into the heterosexual mold of the "good Communist wife."

The status of women in the United States is more complicated. Women who are born to or who marry into families with wealth and privilege are quite free and independent. Also, the emphasis on individualism in America offers a limited number of women the opportunity to excel on their own, becoming "tokens" of power within mainstream institutions or tolerated as unusual or eccentric figures within the margins of society, usually in intellectual and artistic circles.

In the United States, the idea of equality for all women, or what was eventually referred to by the feminist movement as "sisterhood," challenged not only sexism in institutional and personal life but the very foundation of the capitalist system, which is based on inequality and competition, including inequality and competition between women. In that sense, women's liberation was a very radical idea. The feminist movement emerged not because the government or businesses thought it was time to provide more opportunities for women, but because radical activists in the 1960s agitated for change.

Rita Mae Brown stepped into the political arena in 1966, a period when radical activists were focused on obtaining rights for racial minorities and bringing an end to the Vietnam War. "Women" and "gays" were not yet recognized as distinct groups that were in need of movements of their own. But from the start, Brown was ahead of her time. Emboldened by claims to power and pride that were being made by militant blacks in this period, Brown, a college student who had been an "out" homosexual since 1961, helped to form, on behalf of the gay community, an organization similar to some of the more militant groups involved in the black civil rights struggle.

Within a few months of the founding of the Student Homophile League in 1967, Brown established a chapter at New York University. Prior to this time, conservatives and radicals in existing pro-gay organizations, such as the Mattachine Society and the Daughters of Bilitis, had been locked in a dispute concerning the image and strategy of the Homophile movement. Conservative members believed that homosexuality would become acceptable only if gay people projected themselves as well-adjusted, conventional Americans. Alternatively, the radicals focused on societal reactions to homosexuality, targeting the government and the psychiatric establishment as key sources of gay oppression. The Student Homophile League represented the radical view. Many of its members also participated in broader-based protest movements against the Vietnam War and racism.

When the women's movement emerged in the late 1960s, Brown shifted her political priorities. She exited the gay movement once she recognized that, like all the radical social movements of this period, it

In late 1979, Navratilova was reunited with her family when they came to live with her in Dallas. From left are her sister, Jana; her mother, Jana; and her stepfather, Mirek. Difficulties in adjusting to American life and Martina's lesbianism made Navratilova's parents unhappy in the United States, and they returned to Czechoslovakia after a short time.

was dominated by men. Their gayness, in this case, did not make them much less chauvinistic in their attitude toward women. She aligned herself with a small radical feminist group in New York City called Redstockings. Again, even within this radical organization, Brown took a radical position: she challenged the members of the group to express their commitment to women and to sisterhood by leaving men altogether and becoming lesbians—working with, living with, and loving with other women.

This political stance, which has been alternately referred to as "radicalesbianism," "political lesbianism," "lesbian separatism," and "lesbian nation," not only suggests an extreme strategy for combating sexism but implies that people can choose and change their sexual orientation. In 1971, Brown, who had moved from New York to Washington, D.C., helped to form a collective of women who called themselves the Furies. These women were resolved to living—every waking, breathing moment of their existence—according to the principles of radicalesbianism. In its full-blown form, this meant that they lived together; shared everything, including food, money, chores, and even underwear; worked outside the collective in alternative institutions that serviced women only; steered clear of all forms of "male energy," including male children; and promoted lesbianism as the highest form of love and commitment between women.

While today this may sound cultish, if not outlandish, many chroniclers of the women's movement have argued that this political perspective and the women who crafted it provided much of the energy and industry that fueled the more tempered and mainstream feminist organizations that remain in existence to this day.

The Furies disbanded in 1972—in part due to all the rules for living "correctly" that these activist women imposed on themselves and each other; in part due to Brown's penchant for adventure and stirring up trouble, even in the context of a revolutionary, utopian collective; and in part due to the overall decline of radical movements in the 1970s. Moreover, Brown possessed both individual talent and ambition that ultimately could not find expression in the collective identity of a movement activist.

After *Rubyfruit Jungle* was published in 1973, Brown became a celebrity, a heroine in the gay community, and an icon for lesbians. By the decade's end, she had drifted away from social movement politics. In 1979, she recalled in an interview, "I was living on a small farm east of Charlottesville [Virginia], and looking for more land. I love farming and I grew up on a farm." She was also working on her fourth novel, *Southern Discomfort.* "I never anticipated sharing my life with anyone at that time," she remembered. "I am, by nature, a lone wolf."

Given the facts of Brown's history, it is hard to imagine the basis of the bond between this 34-year-old, hypersophisticated, radical lesbian intellectual and the 22-year-old tennis star, who was liberal and sympathetic to feminism and the rights of all minorities but otherwise a jock who exalted the economic opportunities of capitalism and who believed her homosexuality was her own business.

The basis for the bond was not obvious, but it was there. While growing up in different countries, under different political regimes, at different times, both Navratilova and Brown were willful and resilient little girls who became powerful women. They cut loose from their families at an early age in order to pursue lives of achievement that would have been prohibited if they had remained close to home. Both came from economically austere backgrounds. And both had developed a deep appreciation for the material goods and comforts that their successes had brought to them. This last similarity was a critical one: while Brown and Navratilova's individual personalities and interests were merging in a challenging love affair, their mutual love of creature comforts encouraged new heights of material extravagance.

By 1980, Navratilova was already a millionaire. She had earned more money than any other woman tennis player in history. She owned seven sports cars—one for each day of the week. That year, she and Brown moved into a 20-room mansion in Charlottesville. Their secluded home was surrounded by a stone wall, nine acres of farmland, formal gardens, fountains, and statuary. Navratilova installed a swimming pool, universal gym, and tennis court, intending to maintain all the good habits of training and exercise that Haynie had instilled in her. From this home base, the two women proceeded to juggle the requisites of Navratilova's tennis career, Brown's writing career, and their domestic life, which centered on Brown's desire to farm the land they had purchased.

While Brown respected Navratilova's accomplishments, she possessed no great reverence for the world of professional sports, which she referred to as "the last great bastion of those individuals motivated by both greed and nostalgia." She also expressed disdain for the restricted and simple-minded activities—such as playing cards, doing crossword puzzles, thumbing through old magazines, and watching the soaps on television—with which most players killed time on the tour.

In her autobiography, Navratilova describes Brown's efforts to get her out of her hotel room and into the streets, the museums, the theaters, and the bookstores of the cities where she was playing. Initially, Navratilova was thrilled: she developed an interest in architecture, she read more, she socialized with different kinds of people, and she even contemplated the possibility of taking classes and getting a college degree.

At the same time, Navratilova was not about to give up tennis or to settle for anything less than being the top player on the tour, and all the outside stimulation often left her exhausted: "There were times when I'd barely get to the courts in time for my matches. I'd be calling in and saying, 'What time's the match? Who's winning? What's the score?' Occasionally, I'd get there (to the courts) and my feet would be tired from standing in a museum or walking the streets and my mind would be buzzing from a movie we'd seen or a conversation we'd had." And there would be Chris Evert or Billie Jean King standing on the other side of the net waiting to serve.

Moreover, as idyllic as life in the Charlottesville countryside could be, it was not a very convenient place to live for someone who spent as much time traveling as did Navratilova. Often, she had to add an extra two hours to a trip because of the drive from Charlottesville to the nearest major airport, which was in Washington, D.C. And then there was the matter of having to explain to others why she was living in such a remote, rural area in the first place. She did not feel free to come out and say, "I'm indulging my lesbian lover's fantasy of being a citizen-farmer in the tradition of Washington, Jefferson, and Adams,"

A member of London's infamous paparazzi captured Navratilova and Rita Mae Brown returning to their rented apartment during the 1980 Wimbledon tournament.

which was the case. Instead, she shrugged off a meaningless "Why not, it's pretty there."

Clearly, Navratilova was learning the American way of being gay: to keep her work life and her personal life separate and to adhere to a code of silence, vagary, and euphemism regarding love relationships. Mitigating this lesson were her internal sensibilities. Unlike some gay people, she did not hate herself or wish she was straight. On the deepest level, she experienced her sexuality as a natural, innocuous characteristic, like the color of her eyes or being left-handed. She was genuinely perplexed as to why it was such a big deal. And she was not good at lying or hiding.

At the time she began her relationship with Brown, Navratilova certainly had not made a conscious decision to come out as a lesbian. However, her choice to become lovers with Rita Mae Brown, perhaps the most famous lesbian in America, subverted any intention she might have had about keeping her personal life private. In public, the mere appearance of Navratilova with this virtual legend of the feminist and gay liberation movements raised eyebrows and drove reporters wild. When the two women bought the house in Charlottesville, it made headlines in national tabloids. "Martina Buys 500G Mansion with Mystery Companion," read one. More significantly, Navratilova's relationship with Brown made headlines in her private life as well, upsetting two of the most important people she knew: her parents.

In her autobiography, Navratilova explains that around the time her mother was granted an exit visa to go to Wimbledon in 1979, the Czech government had given subtle hints that they might permit the entire Navratil family to emigrate to the United States. During their week together in England, Navratilova told her mother that she totally supported the move.

When Navratilova made this commitment, she had already separated from Haynie, but she was still maintaining a home in Texas. She planned to settle her parents in a house close to hers in Dallas, support them financially, send her sister, Jana, to a first-rate high school, and visit them when she was not on tour. At the time, it seems, she did not give much, if any, thought to how or even if she would disclose the matter of her sexuality to her family.

Her family arrived just in time for Christmas. Things went as planned, at least for a while. Martina provided her parents with two cars, a Peugeot she had won in a tournament and a Cadillac Seville she purchased from Haynie. She furnished their house, complete with modern appliances and a piano. She paid all the bills. She sent Jana to

Navratilova and King compete as a doubles team in a tournament in Japan in 1980. At the time, the press seemed to be as interested in each player's personal life as they were in their tennis.

Hockaday, a private prep school. She visited them as often as she could and invited them to accompany her on tournaments.

Even so, she was not around all that much, and the Navratils had a difficult time adjusting to their new life. They made it clear to their oldest child that they would have preferred it if the entire family lived in the same house. They were not confident in their ability to communicate in English, and when their daughter was away they would call

her, needing help with negotiating simple matters like getting an appliance repaired. When she was with them, they acted like parents, wanting to know all the details of her life, giving her advice, fussing over her. At one point, Mirek, who was not used to being idle, announced that he wanted to resume coaching Martina, something that at this advanced point in her career was just not realistic.

The tension between Navratilova and her parents increased. When, just a few months after her parents' arrival, she became involved with Brown, a full-blown crisis erupted. Initially, Navratilova thought that she would be able to juggle three separate lives: one as a tennis pro on the road; one as the daughter of understandably disoriented parents who had just been transplanted from Prague to Dallas and from a Communist to a capitalist society; and one as the lover of a high-strung, high-powered authoress-farmer in the countryside of Virginia. For a while, she was able to pull it off. As she recounts in her autobiography, "I could afford two houses, plus one for my family, so I didn't think it was any big deal if I lived part of the time in Charlottesville. But when I told them I was buying another house, they didn't love the idea. . . . And then they got the drift of why."

Navratilova's parents' view of homosexuality was consistent with that of Czech Communist society: it is a sickness. They were completely uninformed of the changes in thinking about homosexuality that were occurring in Western societies in the 1970s, including its removal from the official list of psychiatric disorders. Mirek was especially distraught and groped for reasons that, in his mind, would explain what had gone wrong with his daughter. "There must be something wrong with you physically," he said. Or, "The reason you're going through this is because you didn't enjoy the first time you were with a man."

Navratilova's mother took a different, but no less disapproving, view of the matter: she blamed it on Brown, telling her daughter that she was just being used by this woman, that she was too open and too trusting. In the middle of one heated and unpleasant discussion between Navratilova and her parents, her mother compared Martina to her biological father, revealing for the very first time that he was mentally ill and had, in fact, taken his own life.

For most gay people, negative responses from parents—as compared with those from friends, colleagues, or society at large—are often the most devastating. Unusually resilient, Navratilova claimed in her autobiography that even while this crisis was unfolding, she never questioned her parents' underlying love for her. But she was not immune to their condemnations. Her immediate reaction was to appease her parents by softening some of the disclosures she had made to them. She attempted to place her relationship with Brown in a different light, casting it as more of an emotional than a sexual bond. She used the term "bisexual" to describe herself and assured them that she liked to make love with men also. But Mirek did not buy any of it, and neither did Brown.

CHAPTER SEVEN

SEX AS SUBLIMATION FOR TENNIS

When Navratilova's parents visited their daughter's Charlottesville home, Brown refused to indulge the Navratils' homophobic reactions and would not collude in her lover's distortions of their relationship. "The fact that I was not her first lover or even her third or fourth in no way lessened their animosity for me. They blamed me for this dreadful calamity. Of course, they would have blamed anyone," she recalls.

The issue was never resolved. Navratilova's parents became more resentful and critical of everything she did. That they were living in unfamiliar surroundings and completely dependent on her aggravated the situation. This family reunion just was not working out.

In the end, Navratilova's parents decided to return to Czechoslovakia. Apparently, it was primarily Mirek's decision to leave. Brown recalls their departure: "Mirek Navratil couldn't adjust to American life.

The Navratilova backhand. She brought an unprecedented power and athleticism to women's tennis.

[He] could not cope with our country and never let an opportunity slip away to criticize us in florid terms. . . . When he returned to Czechoslovakia he got a lot of mileage from denouncing us." In her autobiography, Navratilova says that their departure left her sad and disappointed, both in them and in herself. She kept wondering if they all could have handled it better. She also had second thoughts about refusing to allow her sister, Jana, to remain with her, as Jana had requested. Despite all the conflicts, once her family had left she missed them right away.

That Navratilova was able to wave good-bye and go on with her life likely has more to do with her resilience than actually being indifferent or unscathed by her parents' reactions. However, this crisis was only a small personal drama compared to the public scandal that was about to unfold in the world of women's tennis. At center stage of this drama was none other than the woman who had created this world in the first place, Billie Jean King.

Marilyn Barnett, a woman who was initially introduced on the women's tennis circuit as King's hairdresser and was later given the title of private secretary, had filed a civil lawsuit claiming entitlement to alimony for a period in the 1970s when she and King had been lovers. The press dubbed it the "galimony" suit.

Needless to say, the officialdom of women's tennis—executives with the Women's Tennis Association and its many corporate sponsors, as well as those among the players who had personal reasons to worry about a gay scandal—were sent into a panic. Reporters sought sensational gossip about illicit liaisons in the women's locker room. Parents of the younger players voiced fear that their daughters might be "lured into lesbianism."

King publicly admitted to having had an affair with Barnett and settled the suit. Yet she steadfastly refused to identify herself as gay, saying, "I don't feel like a homosexual." She even appeared on a talk show hosted by Barbara Walters, holding hands with her long-estranged husband, Larry King, and saying that the affair was "a mistake," an aberration for which she was very, very sorry. She expressed the hope that women's tennis and the organizations that supported the sport would not suffer because of her indiscretion. She even offered to step down as president of the Women's Tennis Association.

The Women's Tennis Association neither expelled King nor fed the flames of hysteria. Instead, they closed ranks and pursued a strategy of damage control. Officials let players know that they would not tolerate another "outing." Moreover, word circulated that Avon Products would withdraw its $4-million-per-year sponsorship of women's tennis if any other player spoke about homosexuality. While there was in all likelihood more than just one top-ranking player who could speak about such matters from personal experience, there is little doubt that these warnings were aimed specifically at Navratilova. The message was clear: if you want to reap the benefits of remaining in the good graces of the tennis establishment—endorsements, positive media coverage, invitations, and awards—you remain in the closet.

This was a very confusing time for Navratilova. She hated lying, and she certainly had a different understanding of her sexual identity than the self-deprecating King. She did not view her attraction to women as "a mistake." In fact, just a few months before the news about the "galimony" suit broke, Navratilova had given an interview to a reporter for the *New York Daily News* in which she identified herself as "bisexual" and discussed her ambivalence about coming out. "If I talk [about having relationships with women], I feel I can be a good example to other people," Navratilova told the sportswriter. "But not now." In the wake of the recent deluge of negative reactions to her way of life—from the Women's Tennis Association and its sponsors, from the press, and from her own parents—Navratilova was having second thoughts. The cost of coming out now seemed tremendously high. At stake were not only her career as a tennis pro and the loss of future millions in corporate endorsements; there was also the possibility that a public disclosure would jeopardize her application for permanent residency in the United States.

By July 1981—after six years of carrying a green card, being detained at passport checks in airports, and having to avoid travel to, through, or over any Communist country where she could be grounded and sent back to Czechoslovakia—Navratilova would have completed the required waiting period for citizenship. Although her lawyers did not anticipate any problems, applicants were routinely asked about their sexual orientation in the citizenship hearing, and homosexuality was still considered a criminal act in many states.

Panic-stricken at the prospect of losing her citizenship, Navratilova asked the *Daily News* reporter not to print the interview in which she had outed herself. The writer agreed to hold off until her citizenship was secured, but he would not kill the story altogether. This meant that in the event that Martina was asked about her sexual orientation at the hearing she would have to tell the truth or else risk perjuring herself under oath.

With her lawyer's advice, Navratilova applied for her citizenship in Los Angeles, rather than in Charlottesville or Dallas, as the laws regarding homosexuality were more relaxed in California than they were in Virginia or Texas. The hearing date was set for the end of May. In her autobiography, Navratilova recounted the event:

> One of the first things I was asked to do was write a simple sentence in English. I wrote: 'The weather in Southern California is wonderful' and that seemed to satisfy them. Then the officer asked me a few questions: What's the color of the flag? Who was the first President of the U.S.? Who is the President now?
>
> Then the officer asked me a few brief questions about whether I had a criminal record or drug habit. There was also something very quick about my sexual identity, and I just gulped and said I was bisexual, and she never even glanced up from the form she was reading. When it was all over she was very friendly but didn't tell me whether I had passed or failed.

The ordeal—more traumatic in the anticipation than in reality—was over. Soon enough, Navratilova learned that her application for citizenship had been been accepted, but she remained confused about making a public acknowledgment of her sexuality.

The impact of homophobia on a gay individual is not something that is readily perceptible or easily measured. Navratilova tended to treat the stress caused by homophobia as temporary and situational, as a distinct event that she must live through, get over, or better yet, ignore. Even so, prejudice and discrimination can and do have chronic and cumulative effects on the self-worth of the individual who experiences them, even on an individual as resilient as Navratilova. The effects of homophobia can also act to destabilize the relationships of gay couples.

Brown's history as a political activist and her career as a writer made her less vulnerable to and less tolerant of homophobia. To someone of Brown's sensibility, remaining closeted for the sake of a sport seemed cowardly. "The only way for it to be safe is for everyone to take the risk. I came out in 1961. No picnic," she says, recalling Navratilova's indecision in 1981. In her opinion, the tennis establishment's fretting over the gay women in their midst was, and still is, unnecessary. "The public is more liberal than the Women's Tennis Association," she argues. "The W in WTA stands for wimp. The King affair didn't keep anyone away from tournaments. So those in charge revealed the depths of their prejudice because the ticket sales did not reflect the doom they predicted if the very word lesbianism was ever breathed publicly. They have learned nothing from that reality. Nothing."

Undoubtedly, in the course of their relationship Brown had imparted some of these thoughts to her lover. Perhaps if Navratilova's parents had been less condemning, or if the King affair had not caused such an uproar, or if her citizenship had not been on the line, Navratilova would have come out in 1981. She had already made it to number one as a tennis player. She was already a millionaire. She was already 24, an age by which many female players retire from the sport. And tennis was, as Brown reminded her over and over again, "only a game."

But on that score, Brown was dead wrong. For Navratilova, tennis is not just a game or a sport or a job. It is a passion, a lifeline, and it ultimately supercedes everything and everyone else in her life. As her relationship with Brown progressed, Navratilova explains in her auto-biography, Brown became more impatient and critical of her compliance to the norms and demands of the tennis world. Navratilova interpreted Brown's continuous critique of the tennis establishment—however accurate—as unsupportive. In an effort to avoid confrontation, she tried to appease her partner. She cut corners on her practice. She played in fewer tournaments. She encouraged Brown to remain home and do her own work while she was on tour, although she would have

Three times an All-American and four times a member of the U.S. Olympic team, basketball star Nancy Lieberman replaced Rita Mae Brown in Navratilova's life.

liked a more supportive partner to accompany her to tournaments and root her on from the friends' box. Eventually, the stress in Navratilova's emotional life was reflected in her tennis.

In 1980, Navratilova failed to make it to the finals at Wimbledon, the U.S. Open, or the Australian Open. Her computer ranking had slipped from number one to number three. At the beginning of the 1981 season, in a tournament on Amelia Island, her performance declined even further.

Navratilova met Evert in the finals, but her game was so far off the mark that at one point in the second set she handed over her racket to a ballgirl, signaling to the crowd that the girl could probably do a better job. Not only did Navratilova lose the match, she lost every game, suffering an embarrassing 6–0, 6–0 defeat, which in tennis lingo is referred to as a "double bagel."

In part, Navratilova's performance on Amelia Island was symptomatic of all the recent stresses in her life. However, there is another explanation for this particular loss. The night before the match, she had not had much sleep—not because she was worrying about her game, but because she stayed up talking, laughing, and watching videos with a new friend.

Known to the sports world and her fans as "Lady Magic," Nancy Lieberman was the first female basketball star in America. She had come to Amelia Island to watch tennis and relax after an especially grueling season with her team in the Women's Professional Basketball League, the Dallas Diamonds. Navratilova had spotted her in the stands while she was playing a match in the early rounds. "In those days," she later wrote, "I was not always concentrating on my matches the way I should. . . . What's she doing here? I thought to myself as I hit a forehand. . . . Who does she know on the tour? I wondered as I hit a smash for a winner." Interested at once, she started asking around for answers to her questions. Later in the week, television announcer Bud Collins introduced them.

In her own autobiography, *Lady Magic*, Lieberman claims that before they met she had no interest in Navratilova, tennis, women's tennis, or women. She was not, as far as anyone knew, including herself, gay. As an avowed born-again Christian, she in fact held religious convictions that viewed homosexuality as a sin. But from the moment she met Navratilova, Lieberman wrote, there was an "instant attraction, an instant level of comfort. . . . Maybe for that particular time in my life, that's what God wanted me to experience. I honestly don't know."

For Navratilova, her attraction to Lieberman was based on an intriguing discordance between her tough, gruff, street-smart manner and her feminine appearance—tall, graceful, and slender, with flaming red hair. For Lieberman, the attraction to Navratilova was in meeting a kindred spirit, another woman who was as interested in sports as she was, someone whom she could trust with things that hurt emotionally, such as her parents' divorce and the lack of attention from her father. Martina was someone who seemed to need her.

At that moment in her life, Navratilova was nothing if not needy. Her tennis career was spiraling downward. She perceived her lover as distant and unsupportive. She was still awaiting the results of her citizenship application. In the near future, the *Daily News* interview would hit the newsstands and there would be some fallout from the tennis establishment. "In some ways," Lieberman wrote of Navratilova, "she was like a helpless baby who needed somebody strong to take care of her. The more we talked the clearer it became that I could be the person in Martina's life to protect her and be strong for her."

After their introduction, Navratilova and Lieberman stayed together all day and into the night. "By the time either of us looked at a clock," Lieberman recalls, "it was 6 A.M. I felt bad because Martina had a championship match at noon and here she was falling into bed at 7 in the morning. As I left, I wished her luck in the match and told her I'd be watching and pulling for her against Chris Evert."

After watching the disastrous match, Lieberman sat in on the post-match press conference. "It was all I could do not to laugh," she remembered, "looking at a grinning Martina as she tried to explain her goose-egg loss. She may have lost the match, but she gained a companion who was going to help her reshape her life and women's tennis for the next three years."

Although Navratilova was still ostensibly living with Brown, she pursued her relationship with Lieberman on the phone and on the road. Lieberman met her at the French Open and at Wimbledon and was even in the courtroom in Los Angeles when Navratilova was sworn in as a U.S. citizen. Eventually, at the house in Charlottesville, Brown overheard a phone conversation between Navratilova and Lieberman: the inevitable scene unfolded and ended with Navratilova grabbing the two items that had come to symbolize the expanse and limits of her life—her tennis racket and her suitcase.

Navratilova described the tumultuous parting in her autobiography:

> Rita Mae watched me put my stuff together, and let's say, she did not take it lightly. She was hurt, anybody would be, and we got into one of the nastiest, most physical arguments I ever hope to be in. We stormed around the house raging at each other, from room to room, until I couldn't take it anymore.
>
> I raced out of the house, getting to the car before she did, and jammed it into gear and spun out of the driveway, spewing gravel and exhaust fumes. . . . I felt numb, dead inside, with no incentive to get about my tennis again. I needed something to shock me into the next stage of my life and Nancy seemed to be it.

Throughout the years they were together and for many years after, Navratilova and Lieberman publicly denied the romantic and sexual component of their relationship. Even in her autobiography, which was published in 1985, Navratilova refers to Lieberman as her "friend," "roommate," and "trainer." In their private life, the relationship was treated as an open secret—people around them "knew" but avoided explicit labels and references.

So far as Brown was concerned, it was no secret at all. "The most accurate characterization of the end of our relationship," she says, "is that [Martina] grew tired of me. The homophobia surrounding us contributed to me becoming less and less alluring and she replaced me with a closet case of risible dimensions. . . . [She] vowed that they would be together until death them did part. That 'the latest' understood her and their physical passion was incinerating. This WAS IT." To insure clarity about the matter, Brown granted an interview to a reporter from the *Washington Post*: the details of the "tearful end" to this "odd love match" appeared on the front page of the newspaper's Style section.

The newly constituted couple feigned disinterest in Brown's disclosures. According to Lieberman, Navratilova told her former lover to feel free to talk to anyone she liked about their relationship: "Go write an article or a book. . . . Knock yourself out—it won't bother Nancy or me." In fact, Navratilova was bothered and upset and bombarded

Always emotional, Navratilova jumps for joy after defeating Chris Evert in the semifinals of the 1981 U.S. Open. Lieberman made a profound difference in the way Navratilova prepared to practice her profession.

with questions from the press as reporters geared up for another sex scandal. This one would involve major stars, with major endorsements in both tennis and basketball.

It was at this point that the lying began. Not only did Navratilova and Lieberman deny that they were romantically involved, but Lieberman went so far as to announce that as part of the training regimen she had set out for Navratilova, which included changes in practice, diet, and exercise, she also intended to change her sexual orientation. "I'm not saying [lesbianism] is wrong," she told reporters at a press conference in Dallas, where the couple made their home, "but I want to give her a fair chance of changing and seeing the other side. I'm not here to force guys on her but just to help her get out of that environment. If you don't know anything else, you can't give it a chance." Having already transformed herself from a Jew to a Christian, Lieberman was no stranger to conversion. But clearly she was not ready to announce or perhaps even admit to herself that she, not Navratilova, had undergone yet one more changeover: from straight to gay. In truth, of course, it was Navratilova who had converted *her,* though she attributes the experience to God. Interviewed separately, Navratilova collaborated in the folly: "I like men, I guess I'm bisexual. . . . Men call me—especially black guys. In fact, I've always had more men calling or writing."

Years later, Brown would characterize these utterances as one of the more "unshining" moments in Martina's life. Even the reporters who recorded the couple's statements seemed suspicious and took pains to preface the disclaimers in the context of the negative reaction Navratilova was likely to receive from the tennis establishment were she to admit to the truth of the relationship, as well as the endorsements both women had to lose if they admitted to being lovers.

Even so, Navratilova's participation in such a blatant distortion of the truth was out of character and begs for some explanation. Left to her own devices, Navratilova prefers honesty. She is, however, rarely left to her own devices: she is terrified of being alone. Although this fear has subsided somewhat with age, she admits, for instance, that since 1978 she has owned a gun, which gives her a sense of security on those nights she spends without a companion. Even in her tennis, she needs someone to be as involved with her performance as she is, someone beyond a coach.

From the moment Navratilova hightailed it out of Charlottesville, Lieberman became that someone. But in contrast to Navratilova's basic acceptance of herself, Lieberman's sense of identity was less stable. In *Lady Magic*, she describes a lifelong struggle with a mother who worried more about social convention and "what the neighbors would think" than about encouraging her daughter to pursue her athletic talent, which was an unconventional interest for a girl at that time. Though her passion for basketball prevailed, she was left with conflicting feelings about being "different" and the need to constantly prove that she was otherwise a "normal" girl. As a result, Lieberman was entirely unable to integrate the relationship she was having with Navratilova into her view of herself and the world. In her autobiography, Lieberman (who now is married to a man) writes about the details of her relationship with Navratilova without ever once mentioning the words gay, lesbian, or homosexual. Even today, Lieberman says that she still does not really understand what happened between the two of them.

Given Lieberman's profound level of discomfort with a gay lifestyle and Navratilova's profound dependence on her, the two seemed to have convinced themselves that they could and should lead a double life. At home they were lovers. In public—at tournaments, at practice, in the press room—Lieberman was the straight trainer who dated men and Navratilova was the bisexual protégée who was contemplating having relationships with men.

A more feminine appearance accompanied the supposed newfound interest in men. Navratilova let her hair grow longer, and she started to use a lightener, changing the color from brown to blond. She wore makeup. Her tennis outfits became brighter and more feminine looking. Her weight had finally stabilized at a trim 145 pounds, down from a high of 167 in the late 1970s. The "new" Navratilova had to be described as nothing short of glamorous. Image was all: more important than actually becoming heterosexual was that she project a heterosexual image, that she look like a woman who cared about being attractive to men.

CHAPTER EIGHT

TEAM
NAVRATILOVA

While smoke and mirrors, a little lipstick, and some lies solved Navratilova's image problem—at least for the moment—her primary concern was repairing her tennis game. In many ways, the relationship between Navratilova and Lieberman was similar to the relationship that she had had with Haynie. The door to the closet where Lieberman hid read "trainer," but the title was legitimate. Lieberman had an in-your-face, drill-sergeant approach to getting Navratilova into shape. She was loud, intimidating, and relentless. "As an athlete," Lieberman observed, "I was shocked by her lack of preparation."

Lieberman goaded Navratilova into waking up early, extending her workouts—which now included weight training and a daily four-mile run—and increasing the amount of time she spent practicing tennis. "I dare you to practice for three hours a day," she would say.

With Lieberman, Navratilova had to adjust to an austere lifestyle. Her home base had moved from the

Dr. Renée Richards prepares to make a return in the semi-finals of the 1976 Tennis Week Open in South Orange, New Jersey. One of the most unusual figures in the history of professional tennis, Richards became an integral part of Team Navratilova.

extravagant Charlottesville mansion to Lieberman's modest townhouse in Dallas, where she was expected to share housework and cook her own meals. Lieberman also confronted Navratilova about her impulsive spending habits, which had gotten out of hand following the breakup with Brown. She explained that confidence was not to be found in a new car or by wearing a diamond ring, nor was love and companionship secured with expensive gifts. By summer's end the media had grown tired of pursuing the couple. All they could see was trainer and protégée hard at work, with Navratilova having set her sights on claiming the one grand slam title that had eluded her: the U.S. Open.

Though New York City was one of Navratilova's favorite places, she had never even made it to the final round of the Open. That year, however, the new Navratilova—who even took the court with ribbons in her hair—was supremely confident. After breezing through the early rounds, she met Evert in the semifinals. Evert had ousted her the year before, but this time it was Navratilova's turn, and she won in three sets.

Her opponent in the finals was Tracy Austin, who as the number-three player in the world was ranked just ahead of her. "I felt so ready," Navratilova said in her autobiography, recalling her entrance onto Center Court in front of 20,000 spectators. "I felt as festive as my orange and yellow shirt, sure that this was the day I'd break through the last 'Can't Win the Big One' barrier."

Navratilova took the first set easily, 6–1, and for the first time in her career she felt that she had the New York crowd behind her—that the spectators understood how important this title was to her and wanted her to win it. But Austin was well aware that Navratilova had played a grueling match against Evert just the day before, and she stayed at the baseline in a conscious effort to extend every point, hoping to tire her opponent. Navratilova put up a fight, but Austin won the second set in a tiebreaker.

In the third and deciding set, Austin picked up the pace. She became more aggressive, and Navratilova began to choke. She lost control and began to swing ferociously. "I was like a baseball hitter trying to hit two home runs with the same swing," she later recalled. But such an approach made it difficult to keep the ball in play, and she started making unforced errors and even missing shots to her forehand, which was generally her strongest return.

According to Austin in her autobiography *Beyond Center Court,* Navratilova started crying even before the match was finished. At match point, says Austin, "she couldn't even see through her tears," and she double-faulted.

Navratilova was devastated. Once again, a loss at the U.S. Open had unleashed a flood of pent-up emotion. But during the ceremony, Navratilova later said, "something marvelous happened." When the announcer called her name for the runner-up trophy, the crowd burst into wild applause. Although there is no way of knowing how many spectators had followed the trials and tribulations of Navratilova's life during the past year, the New York crowd obviously recognized and appreciated a resilient survivor when they saw one. Even though she lost, even though she cried, and even though the winner was a young, attractive, all-American player, Navratilova had become the favorite.

Presented with this unexpected adulation from the stands, Navratilova continued to do what she was already doing: crying. Only now the tears were falling out of happiness. In this New York stadium she felt, for the first time, that she was no longer an "outsider" in America: "They weren't cheering Martina, the bisexual defector. They were cheering me. I had never felt anything like it in my life: acceptance, respect, maybe even love."

To the tough, competitive Lieberman, however, this outburst of sentiment only carried the day so far. From the player's box, she noted every mistake Navratilova made as she choked her way through the second and third sets. The cheers of the crowd did not change the fact that Navratilova had thrown away a match that should have been hers.

Also seated in the player's box was Dr. Renée Richards, a New York physician "with a unique history," as Billie Jean King put it, "in men's AND women's tennis." Dr. Richards was the former Dr. Richard Raskind, a brilliant ophthalmologist who had also been a high-ranked tennis player—captain of his team at Yale University and all-navy champion while serving in the military. However, in 1975, after a lifetime of experiencing acute discomfort with his identity as a man—a condition known as "gender dysphoria"—Raskind underwent hormonal treatment and surgery that transformed him from a male to a female.

The transformation did not lessen Richards's interest in tennis, and after the sex change she decided that she wanted to compete in professional tournaments as a woman. The Women's Tennis Association, however, refused her application. In defense of its position, the WTA argued that despite the surgery and hormonal treatments, she still retained the genetic attributes of a man, including height, bone structure, musculature, and strength. These male characteristics, said the WTA, gave Richards unfair advantages over the other female players.

In 1977, Richards filed a civil lawsuit against the WTA, charging it with sex discrimination. In court, Richards's attorney rebutted the WTA by pointing out that masculinity and femininity, even on a biological level, were not discrete categories. Feature for feature, there were "real" women who possessed the same physical attributes that allegedly gave Richards a competitive advantage. There were "real" women who were over six feet tall; there were real women with highly developed muscles; there were real women with a large bone structure. The WTA's disqualification of Richards therefore was purely discriminatory, argued her attorney, and reflected the establishment's prejudice toward transsexualism and transsexuals, not any justifiable concerns about competition and precedents.

Ironically, Richards was supported by many of the women players whom the WTA claimed they were protecting, including King and Navratilova. In *Second Serve*, her autobiography, Richards recalls that in the midst of her legal battle, at a time when she was being treated as a freak and an intruder, it was Navratilova who went out of her way to be supportive. Richards believes that it was Navratilova's own experiences of discrimination that enabled her to identify with her and helped forge the friendship between the two.

Richards won the suit, took an indefinite leave from her medical practice, and became a full-time professional tennis player. She proved able to apply her keen mental abilities to the game and developed an unusually sophisticated understanding of the technical aspects of tennis,

Navratilova hits a volley during the 1983 U.S. Open, which she won that year for the first time. Her newfound commitment to physical conditioning and mental preparation made Navratilova the dominant player in women's tennis during the middle and late 1980s.

but even so her tenure as a pro was brief. By 1981, Richards was over 40 years old. Despite all the arguments over her alleged physical advantages, she could in fact no longer compete effectively against the top women players. Frustrated at the thought of her knowledge going to waste, Richards sought to impart her tennis wisdom to someone else. Her first thought was of Navratilova.

As Richards watched Navratilova at the U.S. Open in 1981, she noticed two significant problems with her style: "First, she could not hit a backhand drive. Second, she won most of her games through the force of her athletic ability. Her tactical game was not nearly as strong."

Richards approached her and gave her an assessment of the tactical errors she had made. "If you like," she offered, "I can devote myself to helping you win."

"Good," Navratilova said without a pause, "let's get started." In her autobiography, she explained that she was drawn to Richards because "she was older, she was smart, she had a background outside tennis, she spoke several languages, and she knew things that most of us just didn't know." Her conversations with Richards reminded Navratilova that there was a world outside tennis—a world that she had started to explore with Brown but then had largely forsaken in favor of her career.

Navratilova formally hired Richards as coach right after the U.S. Open. Together, Richards and Lieberman were a formidable duo who complemented one another well as what the press soon dubbed "Team Navratilova." Lieberman served Navratilova as a monomaniacal "motivation coach," while Richards offered herself as technical trainer and an interesting, intellectual friend.

Richards and Lieberman accompanied Navratilova to every tournament. They did everything for her, from making travel arrangements to ordering dessert. Over the years, the members of Team Navratilova would change, but Martina had found a way of having the support and companionship she so craved while on tour. Whereas most of the other players traveled with family members—parents, siblings, and spouses—Navratilova had her team. The creation of this unorthodox squad marked a turning point in Navratilova's journey to self-acceptance, a recognition that she would have to blaze a unique path to success. No matter how weird and unconventional Team Navratilova seemed to others, its captain knew that it was right for her.

Team Navratilova went to work on Martina right after the U.S. Open. Richards redesigned her serve, angling it more sharply to force her opponents out of position. As her arms and shoulders grew stronger from weight work, Navratilova was able to add topspin to her forehand and backhand. Before every match, Navratilova and Richards assessed the strengths and weaknesses of her opponent and developed a strategy of stroke combinations that was likely to upset the opponent's game.

"With Renee and Nancy," Navratilova explained in her instructional book, *Tennis My Way,* "I relearned and rethought everything I ever knew about the game. I learned that matches are won on the practice court, in the gym, and in the mind. I was taught that I have to make my practice sessions twice as tough as my matches so that the matches are easy, physically and mentally."

A systematic conditioning program was added to Martina's training regimen. This included stretches, a fast two-mile run every other day, and an explosive high-energy 30-minute workout in the gym, consisting of stationary bicycle riding, weight lifting, arm drills, abdominal work, stair climbing, treadmill running, and jumping in place.

As a result, the 1982 season was the best of Navratilova's career: she won 90 of 93 singles matches, including 41 in a row; finished first in 15 of 18 tournaments; and won more than $1.4 million—a single-season record for the tour that brought her lifetime winnings thus far to $4.6 million. She won all the major tournaments, including the Australian and French Opens and Wimbledon. She reclaimed number one in the computer rankings. Were she able to win the U.S. Open title, she would become only the third woman in tennis history to win a pure grand slam.

"I'm going to win, I know it," Navratilova told one reporter as tournament time neared. She knew that she was in the best athletic shape of her life, but as she began her practice sessions for the Open, she felt strange. She was tired all the time. Her glands were swollen. Her muscles ached. She tried to go on, but for the first time in her life she was really sick. The diagnosis was toxoplasmosis, a relatively rare virus in humans that is contracted through eating food that is not cooked properly or has been exposed to animal bacteria. The virus would eventually work its way out of her system but eventually was not on Navratilova's schedule. She was determined to play in the Open despite her diminished physical capacities.

Keeping her illness a secret, Navratilova made it through the opening rounds to the quarterfinals, where she met her doubles partner, Pam Shriver. Playing superbly, Navratilova took the first set, 6–1, but she was tiring steadily and dropped the second in the tiebreaker. By the final set, her legs were buckling under her and her racket was hardly making contact with the ball. Shriver closed her out easily; once again, the Open ended for Navratilova with her crying under a towel wrapped around her head.

At the postmatch press conference, Navratilova was in an awkward position. Revealing an illness or injury after the fact was not good

sportsmanship, but Lieberman pleaded with her to tell the truth so that her reputation as a player would be salvaged. Hating the idea of people thinking that she had choked yet one more time at the Open, Navratilova reluctantly spoke about the toxoplasmosis. Needless to say, Shriver was not terribly pleased to have her victory diminished by this revelation. Navratilova felt awful and depressed and ended up pushing

Navratilova and Evert leave the court arm in arm following the finals of the 1983 U.S. Open. By that time, Navratilova had gained the upper hand in their on-court rivalry.

herself to join Shriver in the final doubles match a day later—after all, if she was able to play against Shriver, she should be able to play with Shriver. But she played terribly and they lost. When the Open ended, Navratilova finally succumbed to her fatigue, canceled her next tournament appearance, went home, turned on her answering machine, and slept for days.

Meanwhile, another member was added to Team Navratilova. Navratilova and Lieberman had decided that one of the ways to build back strength and prevent this type of thing from occurring again was through proper nutrition. Through a mutual friend, Navratilova met Robert Haas, a nutritionist who specialized in training athletes to eat correctly in order to achieve full potential and peak performance.

The results were evident immediately. Navratilova's percentage of body fat was reduced, and her chronic problems with monthly menstrual cramping—weakened reflexes and irritability—subsided. Although her craving for junk food did not disappear completely, Haas even systematized the ways Navratilova could cheat on her diet, with occasional sweets, a light beer, and a little butter.

The addition of a nutrition specialist to a training team was unprecedented in the tennis world. Nor did Haas hesitate to publicize his success with Navratilova. In his more grandiose moments, Haas claimed that his system of nutritional engineering had turned Navratilova into a bionic athlete. But Navratilova's goals, however ambitious, were a bit more down to earth: at 26, she intended to keep playing professional tennis—and remain on top—for some years to come. Accordingly, she would need to maintain her body in ways that offset the aging process. The Haas diet helped her achieve that goal.

Though the expansion of Team Navratilova worked well for Martina, the teammates began to fight among themselves. Lieberman's in-your-face style got in the way of Richards's reserve. Richards's formal medical training undermined Haas's experiments with biology and chemistry. Each was jealous of the others' influence on Navratilova.

Richards was the first to leave the team. After a few months of successfully coaching Navratilova full time, Richards decided to return to her medical practice. In *Second Serve*, Richards describes the dilemma she faced: "For years I had tried to make a major success in professional tennis; then, when I had decided to give it up and return to medicine, a success had sort of fallen into my lap. I should have been ecstatic, but I kept thinking about medicine. I don't mean that I didn't enjoy the routine of preparation with Martina; it just seemed that I was postponing my inevitable return to ophthalmology. Furthermore, I found myself dreading the plane rides and the hotels in strange places. What a baffling turn of events! . . . I found myself writing a letter of resignation to Martina. In it I explained that I was being drawn back to medicine, and as much as I had enjoyed our winning streak, I wanted to get on with what seemed to be the major current in my life."

Following the 1983 French Open, Navratilova replaced Richards with a former teammate from World Team Tennis, Mike Estep. Training with a man added a higher level of aggression to Navratilova's performance. Estep was also more laid-back than any of the previous members of the team, and Navratilova felt less controlled and tense around him. With Estep's help, Navratilova claimed a stunning victory over Andrea Jaeger at Wimbledon. In her autobiography, Lieberman recalls how she and some friends celebrated Navratilova's victory: "Martina came back to our flat and we were all ecstatic with her win. She was really tired and wanted a hot soak in the tub before we went out for her victory dinner. Somehow we got her to take a bubble bath. . . . Then we opened a magnum of champagne I had brought from France, and with glasses in hand we invaded Martina's bath. We all took our shoes and socks off and stood in the tub to toast her win. We were drinking champagne and pouring it over her head."

Although Navratilova says Estep was the best thing that ever happened to her, she recognized that her win at Wimbledon was the result of the collective efforts of her team. This would also be the case if she were to win the U.S. Open, which remained "the big one" for her—the one title that she had never won.

As she put it, the U.S. Open was the "monkey on her back." In the eyes of many observers, it was also all that stood between her and the mythical title of "greatest female tennis player ever," a distinction that many accorded to Evert.

The showdown took place on Saturday, September 10, 1983; fittingly, Navratilova was matched in the finals against Evert. In her autobiography, Navratilova recalls that before the finals, she and Estep sat in the lounge outside the locker room. Her knees were knocking and she kept telling herself, "I have to do it now. . . . I'll die if I don't." Estep tried to calm her. "Relax," he told her, "you've already won it in your mind. You just have to prove it to everyone else."

That proof required just two sets and 63 minutes. "I was shaking my fist and jumping up and down, shouting: 'Off my back! Off my back!' because I had finally gotten rid of that monkey, that reputation for choking in the Open," she recalled in her autobiography.

As she returned to her chair on the sidelines and packed up her gear, Navratilova anticipated the postmatch interview. She was so euphoric that she imagined herself walking into the press room singing the opening line to the song "New York, New York." But when the cameras arrived, she did what she had always done at the U.S. Open: she cried. Then she paid all her respects—to her opponent for being a great player, and to Estep, Lieberman, and Richards, for all they had done for her. Afterward, Navratilova celebrated at an Italian restaurant in Little Neck with about 30 friends. They toasted her with champagne, and she broke training with some garlic butter and a few other forbidden foods, hoping that Lieberman was looking the other way.

Navratilova's performance in 1983 had been nothing less than awesome. She had won 86 matches while losing just 1; she captured 15 of the 16 tournaments she entered. Her victories included three of the four grand slam tournaments—Wimbledon for the fourth time, the Australian Open for the second time, and her first U.S. Open crown. Beyond the titles and the money—more than $6 million in earnings for the year—the symbolic achievements were accumulating as well. Along with the inevitable accolades touting her as the best ever, she was named the 1983 Associated Press Female Athlete of the Year and was invited to coauthor (with fellow pro Mary Carillo) a how-to book about tennis.

There was also a noticeable shift in the media's portrayal of her. In the past, Navratilova's achievements were always qualified by some less-than-flattering comments about her looks, her lifestyle, her emotionality, and unfavorable comparisons to Chris Evert. Now reporters seemed more willing to extend the boundaries of convention on her behalf and try to capture the complex composite of a woman who did not fit the mold. Navratilova had, said a cover story in *Time* magazine, "a style of her own." She even was the subject of a feature article and modeling centerfold in the fashion magazine *Vogue,* where the accompanying text read: "Martina's transformation from good to great has put her in a class by herself." Her unique physique and idiosyncratic manner, once met with raised eyebrow, consternation, and even ridicule, were now considered acceptable, interesting, even trend-setting.

Most importantly, Navratilova was now the dominant force in women's tennis, and she had every intention of remaining so for a good, long while. However, she seems to have an internal clock that shifts alternately between "work" and "love." After breaking up with Brown at the end of 1981, Navratilova devoted all of herself to tennis. Even if her relationship with Lieberman had not been entirely platonic, romance certainly seemed to have taken a backseat to training and athletic interests. Lieberman had been instrumental in helping Navratilova renew her career. But with that accomplished, Navratilova had grown tired of Lieberman's bossiness and was straining to break free. When their partnership ended in 1984, the pendulum of Navratilova's internal clock was to shift from work back to love.

CHAPTER NINE

MARTINA GETS MARRIED

Judy Nelson was living in Texas with her physician husband of 15 years, Ed, and their two sons, Eddie and Bales, when she first met Navratilova. Nelson's background reads as a tale of the classic southern belle, with a slight twist of independence and feminism thrown in. She was a 36-year-old graduate of Texas Christian University, a former beauty queen, a dedicated wife, mother, and daughter in a close-knit middle-class Dallas-based family. She had worked all her adult life, at first helping to support her husband through medical school and eventually becoming owner and manager of a Bonanza Steak House franchise.

Judy and Ed Nelson's marriage had been unstable since the late 1970s, although by 1982 the couple had pieced their relationship tenuously back together. As it happened, Nelson was introduced to Navratilova by her son Bales, who was serving as a ball boy during a tennis doubles tournament in Fort Worth. The two women chatted briefly about tennis, politics, and kids and exchanged addresses and phone numbers, agreeing to stay in touch.

Judy Nelson watches Navratilova compete at Wimbledon in 1988.

In Sandra Faulkner's book *Love Match,* Nelson acknowledges that she was immediately attracted physically to Navratilova: "She was easy to talk to and had a great smile and quick wit. . . . Her hair was soft brown with some blond highlights. And her body was the best I had ever seen . . . slender, athletic with well-defined muscles, smooth and tight. Her legs were to die for, and she had the prettiest hands I had ever seen. The skin was soft and flawless and her grip was firm. I admired the way she shook my hand and looked me right in the eye."

Certainly, heterosexual women can and do admire other women. Indeed, despite enduring societal taboos concerning homosexuality, many people experience homosexual or at least "homo-emotional" aspects in their close relationships with individuals of the same sex, without necessarily acting on these feelings or defining themselves as "gay." Moreover, by 1984, when the two met again, Navratilova was not just "any" woman. "She was," as Faulkner puts it, "'MARTINA'—a household name, a multi-millionaire, the number one tennis player in the world." Power and stardom often generate attractions and energy that transcend gender altogether.

Initially, there was no reason for Nelson to impute great meaning to the attraction she felt during her 15-minute conversation with Navratilova. However, nearly two years later, after the two reconnected in Dallas over a lunch of chicken salad sandwiches and Navratilova gave her a good-bye kiss on the cheek, Nelson headed straight for a telephone and called a friend who was also a psychiatrist. "Karen, I need to see you on a professional basis, because either I'm going crazy or I'm going to be the most interesting case you've had in a long time," Faulkner quotes her as saying in that conversation.

Judy Nelson is not the first woman to have had the experience of living all of her adult life as a seemingly well-adjusted heterosexual and then meeting someone who unveiled the "other side" of the sexual continuum. This might have been the basis of Lieberman's confusion as well (although given her capacity for denial, it is possible that Navratilova was not her first homosexual encounter). But in contrast to Lieberman, who "split off" the experience from the rest of her self and her life, Nelson immediately sought to figure out what her feelings meant.

There are two possible explanations for Nelson's feelings. The first holds that the experience unleashed feelings that were there "all along" but remained repressed by societal taboos and lack of opportunity. The second is based on a view that sexuality is more fluid than most people think and that sexual and emotional needs change in the course of the life cycle, which may lead to experimentation or a complete change in sexual orientation. Nelson maintains that she had "no inkling of her homosexual feelings before Martina and that her feelings were focused completely on Martina, not women in general." However, in hindsight she connects her attraction to Navratilova to a long-standing sense of powerlessness she felt as a woman in society and in her marriage. A lesbian relationship presented greater potential for equality.

Nelson was not the only one who was treading on new emotional ground. To the extent that Navratilova had panicked about her own homosexuality in 1981 and was relieved to be with someone such as Lieberman, who was so closeted, her feelings for Nelson reaffirmed the unalterability of her sexual orientation. This relationship required her to take responsibility for who she was and what she wanted. After all, she was bringing Nelson "out" and taking her away from all the conventions and security of a heterosexual family. For the first time, Navratilova was taking the active role.

Nelson heightened the tension in an already dramatic relationship by asking Navratilova to stay in her home with her unsuspecting husband and sons. This rather brazen arrangement allowed the two to secure time together while Nelson continued to play wife and mother and sort out her feelings. Moreover it set the stage for the unfolding of a classic romantic tale: the illicit affair is discovered by the husband, who becomes irate and throws the houseguest out of the house. The lovers cannot stand to be separated, and the wife quickly makes her decision, throws her previous life and all of its assumptions to the wind, and goes off into the sunset with her new amour.

In this case, the sunset was on Amelia Island, where Navratilova was scheduled for yet another showdown with Evert. Nelson sat in the

Nelson congratulates Navratilova after another Wimbledon victory.

players' box, watching the first of what would be many final matches, as Navratilova directed all the energy that is generated from a new love into her tennis. Playing "for" Nelson, Navratilova beat Evert, 6–2, 6–0.

Classic as the story line of this affair was, issues of gender roles and sexual orientation gave it a modern and complex twist. While Nelson had made the decision to relinquish her role to her husband, she had made no such decision regarding her role as mother to her sons. Therefore, she and her new lover had to invent arrangements to accommodate not just their own needs, but those of her children as well.

As Faulkner points out, Navratilova's enormous wealth and generosity made the task possible but still not simple. Eddie, the older son, chose to stay at his father's house. Bales lived with his mother and maternal grandparents in a condominium, while Navratilova lived in a house nearby and Nelson shuttled between the two residences. When Navratilova was on tour, Nelson almost always accompanied her, leaving her sons with their father or her parents when they were in school and giving them carte blanche to meet her and Navratilova—anytime, anyplace—whenever they had free time. Airline tickets were produced for the asking, and private planes were chartered if necessary. Sometimes, Nelson would even fly back to Dallas just for a few hours to participate in some special event at her sons' school. Vacation time was spent in an extended family gathering—Navratilova, Nelson, Nelson's parents, her children, and, frequently, the boys' friends—at a villa Navratilova had purchased on the Caribbean island of Antigua.

In November 1984, after being together constantly for eight months, Navratilova and Nelson decided to formalize their relationship. They purchased rings, found a Methodist church in Brisbane, Australia, and in total privacy—save for the eyes of God—"got married." Faulkner describes the ceremony: "They walked down the empty church aisle and faced each other. . . . The promises were quite traditional—lacking only the presence and words of a minister—but they each vowed to be faithful for the rest of their lives, 'til death do them part. Their commitment vows were essentially the same as those of a heterosexual couple. . . . With the words spoken and promises made, Judy and Martina walked back up the aisle. Just as they opened the doors to go outside, the church bells began to chime, as if on cue." Nelson's sons, according to Faulkner, loved Navratilova. They thought of her as family and accepted the relationship, expressing no need to attach a label to it. Even so, when Nelson revealed the news of the marriage, they were astonished: "Mom, you married Martina? Oh come on, Mom, you MARRIED her?"

As Nelson told it to Faulkner, the relationship between herself and Navratilova was little different from the traditional relationship between man and wife. Nelson willingly and expertly carried out the wifely role. In turn, Navratilova appears to have done everything within her power and means to provide Nelson with assurances of her commitment. Their church "wedding," for example, occurred in deference to Nelson's wishes for a traditional ceremony in the faith in which she was raised. She provided Nelson with a lifestyle—homes, vacations, travel, gifts, and luxuries—that well surpassed the upper-middle-class lifestyle she had enjoyed with her husband. She also took her responsibilities to Nelson's sons seriously, acting as something between a parent and a friend. She taught them to ski, she negotiated disputes, and she took her turn driving in the school car pool. She also extended herself, both emotionally and financially, to Nelson's parents, who, after their initial shock, played a key role in facilitating a joint custody arrangement regarding the children and their parents.

But no matter how traditional and workable Navratilova and Nelson's relationship seemed in private, it was still a nonrelationship in the eyes of the law. Texas law was particularly oppressive regarding gays. Therefore, if anything were to happen in the relationship that required a legal resolution—an illness, a death, a breakup, a custody battle—the partnership would have no legal standing.

With this in mind, the lovers asked a friend who was a paralegal, BeAnn Sisemore, to draw up a nonmarital cohabitation agreement. This document essentially established Navratilova and Nelson as business partners who agreed to combine their earnings. In the event that the partnership dissolved, all the money that remained would be divided evenly. "The monies which either of them may receive as income," the agreement stated, "will be shared by them jointly. . . . Any proceeds remaining from such earnings of either party after any date in which either party may desire to terminate this agreement by separation, shall be the joint proceeds of the parties, to be equally divided." The signing of this agreement was videotaped.

From a purely business angle, given the gross differences in their earning capacity, Navratilova had given away the store. But she was generous, she was in love, she and Nelson had lived quite happily for two years already, and she believed they would be together forever.

Nelson became a constant in Navratilova's personal and professional life. They traveled on the tennis circuit—typically for nine months out of the year—as a couple. While Navratilova practiced, trained, and competed, Nelson coordinated arrangements for a new and expanded Team Navratilova, which now resembled a kind of extended kinship network. At any given moment the team might include Navratilova, Nelson, their friends, Nelson's sons and their friends, Nelson's parents, an array of athletic professionals, including a coach, a trainer, a masseuse, and an osteopath, and an administrative support staff of agents, publicists, and financial managers. Whenever possible, Tets, Puma, Ruby, Yoni, and K.D.—Navratilova's "dogtourage"— joined the team also.

Nelson supervised all the travel arrangements. Wherever the airplane carrying Team Navratilova touched down, the routines were more or less the same. A caravan of limousines, cars, and vans shuttled the team from the airport to a luxury hotel or a rented villa or condo, which would be equipped with phones, Xerox and fax machines and computers, the couple's personal bedding—comforters, pillows, and a featherbed (which Martina and Judy carted with them)—a week's supply of health food, dog food, clothes, and the various personal items belonging to visiting friends and family members.

For the duration of a tournament, Navratilova operated on a tight work schedule. The team could just assume that she would make it to the final or semifinal match of every tournament she played. Practice time, business meetings, press conferences, and public appearances were arranged in advance. It was Nelson's job to protect Navratilova from all unnecessary distractions and see to it that she had time to relax. If there were a few free hours left in the day or evening, the couple would try to enjoy some private time or an outing to a show, restaurant, or cultural event.

During her matches, the entire team occupied Navratilova's friends' box in the stadium, watching her performance, cheering her victories, and consoling her after losses—although in the years between 1984 and 1988 there were very few losses. Members of the team also ran interference between Navratilova and her fans, who clamored for autographs, a greeting, or even a glimpse of the star. Each year, this constituency grew larger and more committed.

Between tournaments, Navratilova traveled to various locations in order to fulfill endorsement commitments. Again, Nelson was almost always by her side. When time allowed, the couple returned to their plush art-deco designer house on Roaring Springs Road in Fort Worth or vacationed in Antigua or on the ski slopes of Colorado.

Nelson's presence and mastery of the wife/manager role created a mobile but stable domestic environment for Navratilova amid her incredibly hectic and demanding public life. For the first time in the history of professional sports, the constant presence of a same-sex partner was not covered up with the title of agent or hairdresser or trainer. Although Nelson and Navratilova did not put a label on their relationship, they went about their business openly and matter-of-factly. Their "marriage" was on display for all the world to see.

But Navratilova and Nelson's openness did not mean that the world at large was ready to accept their relationship. Their appearance together at Wimbledon in 1984, for example, had sent the scandalmongering British press into a frenzy. Reporters knocked on the door of their villa early in the morning and late at night. They followed the couple everywhere, asking inappropriate questions and fishing for personal revelations. Even American reporters whom Navratilova had known and trusted in the past treated the relationship as a "sensation." Frank Deford of *Sports Illustrated* wrote an article in which he insisted that Nelson had been blowing kisses to Navratilova during a match, "something," says Martina, "none of my friends or family would ever consider doing."

Then there were the occasional comments from Navratilova's peers —and even sometimes her friends—that, intentionally or not, fanned the flames of homophobia, such as Evert's quip that Martina "was not the kind of person you would go to with marital problems." Another widely publicized comment was made by Hana Mandlikova, a Czech national. When asked in a postmatch interview about her loss to Navratilova in the final of the 1984 French Open, she replied, "It's hard playing against a man. I mean Martina."

Even Navratilova's good buddy and doubles partner, Pam Shriver, felt obliged to pander to prejudices against homosexuality. "Personally,

Navratilova in action in 1984 at Roland Garros Stadium, site of the French Open. During the mid-1980s, she was invariably seeded number one at all the grand slam events.

I don't care what Martina chooses to do in her private life as long as she is healthy and happy," she wrote in her autobiography. "But in the back of my mind, I think about her meeting the right guy and being swept off her feet. Martina is extremely sweepable. I think it is only a matter of time before she gets married and has kids." Not only did such a comment imply that homosexuality was a lesser option to heterosexuality but it rendered Navratilova and Nelson's relationship invisible and insignificant.

Perhaps the cruelest comment of all was made by Margaret Court, the former tennis great, who said that Navratilova's homosexuality made her a very poor role model for young people, including young tennis players. That Court was one of the players on whom Navratilova had modeled herself made her statements particularly painful.

Within the private everyday life of the circuit, there was much greater acceptance of the relationship. In *Hard Courts,* his book about professional tennis, John Feinstein describes a tour social event in which the players put on a kind of talent show. The performance involved switching identities and mocking each other's quirky mannerisms and habits. In one scene, Robin White played Navratilova, who in turn acted the part of Nelson. "Navratilova did a good job as Nelson," Feinstein observed, "wearing one of her trademark hats and explaining to the audience that she knew more about tennis than any of Martina's various coaches. Each time White, as Navratilova, answered a question, Navratilova, as Nelson, would rush onstage, fix her makeup, and comb her hair. It was perfect." However, it was not the players' acting that impressed Feinstein but the acknowledgment of Nelson as Navratilova's significant other and Martina's ease in this situation.

However, in the public realm—more specifically in the suites of corporate sponsors—Navratilova's image remained a source of concern. The fact is that she received far fewer endorsement offers than one would expect of an athlete of her stature, fewer, for example, than her contemporary Chris Evert. "It's sad," Navratilova told Michelle Kort in an interview in *Ms.* magazine. "It gets to the highest level [of the corporation] and then its: Oh, isn't she gay? Or, hasn't she had relationships with women? Or, isn't she living with a woman? The president of the corporation may be my best friend, but he still won't take that chance. . . . I'm just too controversial."

Some part of Navratilova still craved unconditional acceptance. "Anybody who tells you that they don't want to be loved is either lying or not a nice person. Everyone wants people to know that they're wonderful," she admitted to Feinstein. But gradually, she was coming to grips with the notion that some people would never understand or accept her and that she did not want to be loved for something that she was not. At this point in her career, she did not need to be loved by *everyone*. She was financially invulnerable. The companies that did choose to sponsor her were supportive and loyal. She was adored by legions of fans—gay and straight. A few homophobic executives, a few patronizing remarks from her peers, a few spectators yelling "Martina is a dyke," could not change the fact that Navratilova was the top female tennis player in the world.

"It took me a long time to realize that there's no way I can change people who are going to put labels on me because of my personal life," she told Feinstein. "If someone wants to be a homophobe, that's their right. I can't change them. I feel sorry for people like that, because what scares them is the unknown. . . . It's no different than racism."

CHAPTER TEN

THIRTY-SOMETHING

Between 1982 and 1986, Navratilova was ranked number one in the world each year. Each year she was said to be having the best year of her career; each year the best got better.

In 1985, *Sports Illustrated* characterized her as simply "too good." Wimbledon had become something of her own personal tournament: in 1986, she won her seventh championship there. That same year she captured the U.S. Open for the third time and won 13 of the 17 tournaments she entered. "I remember thinking," Billie Jean King recalled of 1986, "that Martina's play bordered on the unreal."

In 1986, Navratilova turned 30, old age by the standards of professional sports, particularly by those of women's tennis. Speculation about how much time and how many titles were left for her began to appear in accounts of her latest victory. However, Navratilova belongs to a generation of women that, influenced by the aspirations of the feminist movement, refuses to accept biology as destiny. Some of these women push themselves physically by pursuing occupations that

Navratilova's openness —both in displaying her emotions on the court and in her candor about her personal life—is one of the qualities that has made her such a compelling public figure.

During the mid-1980s, Navratilova and Pam Shriver made a nearly unbeatable doubles team. Although Shriver has made an occasional critical public comment about Navratilova, Martina has not held a grudge.

require hard physical labor; some challenge conventional assumptions about childbearing by having first babies at age 40 and beyond; many work out regularly, viewing their bodies as entities that can be sculpted and redesigned, independent of male desire and reproductive function.

Navratilova had been experimenting with her body since 1980, trying to expand her physical capacities—for endurance, coordination, strength, and speed. Although she was not the first female tennis pro to train (in the 1920s, Suzanne Lenglen had lifted free weights), she is responsible for setting new standards of athletic fitness and versatility among her contemporaries. As a result of her training—and with the help of "a great set of genes," as she likes to add—at age 30 she was able to slow her biological tennis clock, rendering the transition from peak to decline almost imperceptible and making everyone wonder whether there would ever be an end at all.

At 30, Navratilova also fretted less about her image and what others thought. She was not Evert and no longer strove to be. "I'm not the girl next door," she told *Ms.* magazine. Gradually, a more authentic Navratilova emerged, as evidenced by her changed appearance. Her new look accentuated her natural athleticism. It included less jewelry, no makeup, androgynous clothing, sharp-edged haircuts, rippling muscles, and protruding veins on her arms and legs.

In 1993, Navratilova would take this look a step further by playing at Wimbledon in shorts instead of a tennis skirt, an unprecedented departure from tennis decorum. Clearly taken aback by this break with tradition, television commentator Bud Collins kept referring to Navratilova's "statement shorts" and anxiously asked his partner in the broadcast booth, Chris Evert, whether Navratilova would be wearing shorts at the upcoming U.S. Open as well. Evert chuckled, with the confidence of someone who had successfully struggled to understand and accept her close friend's "alternative" sensibilities. "Bud," she responded, "I don't think we're going to see Martina play in a skirt ever again."

While some observers characterized Navratilova's look as "ambiguous"—meaning ambiguously female, or somewhere in between female and male—to those familiar with lesbian culture, the look was not ambiguous at all. Navratilova was simply becoming more "butch"—expressing an identity that may appear to the straight world to be mannish or boyish but is really not about men at all. The butch look on a woman is meant to communicate to others that she is a woman who is independent of men and to suggest that she is emotionally and sexually available to other women. Navratilova fused this lesbian-derived identity with her athleticism and designer clothes, putting butch into a higher income bracket and popularizing the look to the point where it was recognized as a distinct fashion that the media dubbed "lesbian chic."

To understand that the butch is not a woman who would rather be a man but rather one who poses an alternative way of being a woman is crucial to understanding why someone like Navratilova, despite her look, was also so emotionally expressive. For years, the tennis establishment just could not—or would not—get it: why this woman who looked so "masculine" lacked a killer instinct; why she so often choked at a crucial moment in a match; why she cried more, hugged more, and cared more than most of her girlish-looking contemporaries. But as Navratilova matured in their midst, the tennis establishment, especially her peers, grew to appreciate her emotionality as a strength and an endearing asset to their sport.

Indeed, Navratilova was extremely popular with her fellow players, many of whom have spoken publicly about her kindness and consideration. In *Passing Shots,* Pam Shriver recounted how moved she was by Navratilova's graciousness after their match at the 1982 U.S. Open. Heartbroken over perhaps her most bitter defeat, Navratilova yet managed to leave Shriver a note in the locker room: "Pam, Congratulations. You played well and since you already beat me, win the tournament. You can do it. Martina." When Navratilova fared better, Shriver noted, she was a great and gracious winner. She would plan victory dinners for 10 or more and be quick to pick up the check for her own celebration. Tracy Austin attests to a similar generosity on Navratilova's part. In 1989, when a car accident forced Austin to watch the U.S. Open from a wheelchair, Navratilova interrupted her own victory ceremony to ask the audience to remember Austin with a round of applause. "How nice that was of her," wrote Austin in *Beyond Center Court,* "but that's just the way she is."

Navratilova's kindness made Hana Mandlikova come to regret the crack she had once made about "playing against a man." As Mandlikova explained in her autobiography, *Hana,* she was moved by Navratilova's response when she finally summoned up enough nerve to apologize for the slur. "I'm not very good at holding grudges," Navratilova said, "and I've been told in the past that I am too lenient with people. Hana, you are the other way. It takes you a long time to trust anyone and then if you get hurt, you have the memory of an elephant. I don't forget—but I do forgive. I forgive you because no matter what happens, I have always felt a kinship towards you." Two years later, when Mandlikova was going through a crisis of her own, Navratilova was the one she turned to for support.

No one attests more to Navratilova's loyalty as a friend than her long-standing rival, Chris Evert. Over 16 years of genuine on-court competition—80 matches and 10 exchanges of the number-one ranking—and a largely media-manufactured off-court rivalry, Navratilova managed to melt the "ice princess." After matches, Evert told one reporter, "We would both go back to the locker room. One of us would be crying. The other would be comforting. Martina has probably seen me cry more than anybody." Over the years, Evert came to realize that Navratilova was indeed someone she could approach with her problems, even marital ones. In fact, it was Navratilova who introduced Evert to her second husband, Olympic skier Andy Mill.

Recognition of Navratilova's uniqueness was not restricted to the members of her own generation. Some of the most important players among her predecessors, including Billie Jean King, Althea Gibson, and Alice Marble, have said that among all the younger pros, they see themselves most in Navratilova, as a champion who wears her heart on her sleeve. In watching the expressive Navratilova ride the highs and lows of her career and personal life, these elders reconnected to the struggles they experienced.

As in tournament after tournament the cameras zoomed in on the victorious Navratilova, the public had little choice but to acknowledge that the best women's tennis player ever looked butch and was married to another woman. Though difficult to measure, the impact of Navratilova's high profile on society was nevertheless significant: everyone who followed women's sports, watched tennis on television or in person, or simply read the sports pages, knew someone who was gay. They knew Martina.

For gay people, and especially for lesbians, Navratilova was—and is—a heroine. Simply by being open about her personal life, Navratilova broke through a barrier of stigma and shame on their behalf. Some of the more radical members of the gay community criticized her for not being outspoken enough, urged her not just to be gay but to proclaim it for all the world to hear, but among the apolitical, the unjaded, and the jocks in the lesbian community, Martina's "being" was enough to send them traveling around the globe, waiting on long ticket lines, and hovering around the entrances of tennis stadiums where she was scheduled to play.

At the age of 30 Navratilova was a magnificent athlete, an admired colleague, an "alternatively" stunning woman, and, Margaret Court's narrow-minded convictions notwithstanding, a terrific role model for all women. Not yet political, in the sense of making statements or holding herself up as a symbol, she nevertheless possessed an explosive, incalculable form of political power—that which comes from living openly within the truth. But before being able to claim fully her rights and publicly proclaim her pride as a gay person, Navratilova would first have to undergo another experience of reconciliation simply as a person.

In the nearly 11 years since Navratilova had left her homeland, her defection had had a positive impact on other Czech tennis players. Fearful of the "next Martina," the Czech Tennis Federation had become more lenient with their top athletes, permitting them to keep more of their earnings and allowing them out of the country for longer periods of time. Hana Mandlikova, six years younger than Navratilova, was probably the Czech player who benefited most directly from the changes in the system that Navratilova's defection had created. She had been able to live in the United States for years at a time and even maintain a residence in Florida.

But Navratilova herself remained a nonperson in the eyes of the Czech bureaucracy. No official record of her achievements existed. At the Revnice Tennis Club, where she had held her first tennis racket, and at the Sparta Sports Arena, where she had trained, there were posters of Jimmy Connors, Bjorn Borg, and Chris Evert, but not Navratilova. Her matches were never televised, with the exception of the 1980 U.S. Open semifinal, when she lost to Mandlikova. Even her predefection feats, such as helping Czechoslovakia win the 1975 Federation Cup, were wiped off the books.

In early 1986, Navratilova applied for a visa in order to visit her family and "get over the shock of being away for ten years." But her application was denied, with the chief of the Passport and Visa Office at the Czech embassy in Washington being quoted in American newspapers as saying, "Navratilova? No way. She left Czechoslovakia without permission. There is no way for her to go back."

When, later that same year, Navratilova was named a member of the U.S. team that had been invited to Prague to compete for the Federation Cup, the Czech authorities had little choice but to relent, however.

Navratilova clowns with Evert and Hana Mandlikova while meeting the press before the 1985 Virginia Slims Tournament in New York City. Year in and year out, Navratilova has been one of the most popular players on the women's tour with her colleagues.

Czech officials made it clear that she was coming as an American and would be treated as an unknown foreigner, yet from the moment she arrived in Prague she was besieged by mobs of adults and kids wanting her autograph. Despite the government's official stance, "everyone knew about Martina," Mandlikova explained. "They had seen her on German television, which Czechs can pick up, or else heard about her on foreign language broadcasts." As far as the Czech people were concerned, says Mandlikova, "Martina had come home. They were joyous that after all these years they were able to share the company of this great champion."

"The most amazing thing," Navratilova told one reporter, "was that I was signing pictures people had cut from magazines 11 or 12 years ago. I couldn't believe anyone had kept them. A couple of guys gave me roses and one little boy gave me a silver pendant with an angel on it. . . . I think I gave them [the Czech people] hope that you can achieve something when you really believe in it. People could lose themselves in what I had accomplished. I was like a fantasy for them. . . . I did what so many of them wished they could do, I made it. It was not just because I left Czechoslovakia, but because of the way I lived, the way I went after my convictions. . . . I never denounced where I came from, or the people. It was just the System that I turned my back on."

At the opening of the Federation Cup competition, Navratilova received a rapturous ovation from the crowd. Not surprisingly, she wept openly when the band played the Czech national anthem, which is entitled, "Where Is My Home?" As captain of the host Czech team, Hana Mandlikova addressed the crowd and welcomed Navratilova home by name. "It was not in the script, but it seemed the logical thing to do," she recalled in her autobiography. "At first I pronounced the name as you do in the West (Nav-ra-til-OH-va) and the people cheered; but the volume was turned up full blast when I repeated my welcoming address in Czech (Nav-ROT-ee-lo-va)."

"Martina," observed Mandlikova, "was more than a mere tennis player. She was a torchbearer coming home." Although she did not say much to reporters during the competition, encouraging them to interview her teammates instead, "her presence," said Mandlikova, "spoke volumes."

Czech officials, meanwhile, did everything to mute the impact of her visit. They scheduled the U.S. team's first match against China on a small court near the railway line that could accommodate only a fraction of the spectators who could be seated at Center Court at the new Stvanice Stadium, where the Soviet Union met Bulgaria. While the Soviets and the Bulgarians volleyed in front of thousands of empty seats, fans fought for position in order to catch a glimpse of Martina. According to Billie Jean King, "even the trains on the railway slowed down as they passed so that passengers and crew could look out the windows and savor a few moments of history." Later on, when Navratilova played a singles match against Mandlikova, the stadium announcer, following official policy, introduced Navratilova only as a "top-ranked player from the United States" and refused to say her name. Mandlikova threw down her racket and refused to play until the announcer introduced her opponent by name. According to Mandlikova, cheering for Navratilova was one of the few ways the Czech people could publicly express their disapproval of the government.

Delighted by the reception given her by her former compatriots, Navratilova still found her stay difficult. The harassment by government officials—secret police followed her and Team Navratilova everywhere—reminded her of why she had been forced to leave Czechoslovakia in the first place, and she did not stay one day beyond the time it took her to lead the United States to a Federation Cup victory.

Four years later, when Navratilova came back to play in another Federation Cup tournament, she returned to a much different Czechoslovakia. More than seven decades of Communist rule in the Soviet Union were coming to an end, enabling the nations of Eastern Europe to move toward greater autonomy. In late 1989, a coalition of intellectuals, students, labor leaders, and activists of every stripe, under the leadership of Vaclav Hável, an internationally renowned playwright and Czechoslovakia's best-known dissident, carried out what became known as the "Velvet Revolution." While strikes paralyzed the economy, massive demonstrations took place in Prague's Wenceslas Square

Navratilova's 1986 visit to Prague marked her first return to her homeland since her defection in 1975. Here, she is flanked by her parents in an appearance on Czech television.

virtually every day. After 24 days the Communist government fell, completing what one observer described as the "fastest, merriest, improvisational—and peaceful" revolution in history. Czechoslovakia became a democratic, independent republic, and Havel was elected its first president.

Navratilova returned to Prague just six months after the revolution. "The contrast between Martina's first return in 1986 and her second visit in 1990 was remarkable," observed Judy Nelson, who accompanied her on both trips, in *Love Match*. This time, she was free to come and go as she pleased. She and Nelson returned to Revnice, where they threw a block party. Together, they visited the grave site of her biological father and the cemetery where her Grandmother Subertova's ashes had been spread after her death in 1979, at a time when there had been no way for Navratilova to return for her funeral.

Officially, Navratilova had been restored to personhood by the new liberal government. Her name was again placed in the record books, her picture was put on the walls of all the sports clubs, and her matches were televised regularly. Perhaps the most exciting event of this return visit occurred when she and Nelson coincidentally ran into Vaclav Hável at a restaurant in Prague. Still improvising, Hável invited Navratilova to address an election rally in Wenceslas Square.

From a balcony overlooking the square, Navratilova addressed more than 200,000 of her countrymen in her native tongue. "It's nice to be a person again," she said. The crowd exploded into a roar. When their cheering finally subsided, Navratilova hesitated. "I am overwhelmed. I will cry if I continue," she added.

Navratilova did a lot of crying on this trip. "Some real serious emotional things came up," she said to a reporter for the *Washington Post*. "A lot of baggage from Czechoslovakia. My parents. My grandmother's death." Reconnecting with all the people and memories she had been so completely cut off from since her defection "was wrenching," she said. "I guess because it's a free country now you're allowed to feel more."

CHAPTER ELEVEN

SAYING GOOD-BYE

"I always said I'd play tennis until I'm 30 and then I'd see," Navratilova once said to a reporter. In 1987, at the age of 31, she was still "seeing." But the year started out miserably, with six losses in the six events she played, including the Australian and French Opens. People close to her tried to account for the sudden plummet. Billie Jean King commented, "When you're used to winning all the time, it's like a pressure cooker, the steam building and building. When you lose, it lets all the steam out and you have to start over again." Others believed that Navratilova had reached an unprecedented plateau and just did not know how to deal with it. Still others marked this as the beginning of the end of her career. "We're seeing a sunset," said Ted Tinling, a longtime official in the WTA, "and sunsets are a beautiful thing to behold."

Navratilova was growing older, of course, and at a time when an extraordinary group of young, talented

Navratilova's many dogs were a frequent part of her traveling entourage. Here, she walks them outside the Paris hotel where she was staying while competing in the 1988 French Open.

players was coming into its own. Including Arantxa Sanchez of Spain, Gabriela Sabatini of Argentina, Steffi Graf of West Germany, Helena Sukova of the Czech Republic, and the sisters Manuela and Katerina Maleeva of Bulgaria, this younger generation was taller, stronger, fitter, and hit with much greater power than the players of Navratilova's generation. They also brought to the court a single-minded determination to dethrone the reigning champion.

Navratilova herself was growing doubtful about whether she still had what it took to win. During a match, her state of mind could shift from arrogance to panic in an instant. Reporters noticed that on the court she was easily distracted, by the noise of an airplane, say, or a seagull squawking overhead. "I know there is nothing wrong with my game. There's nothing wrong with me technically. At this point it's all emotional. It's in my head," she told a reporter for the *New York Times*. But, she was quick to add, "I'm not finished yet." She scrambled to fix the situation. She changed rackets, from Yonex to Dunlop, and coaches, from Estep to Randy Crawford to Tim Gulliksen. She even asked for help from Renée Richards and Nancy Lieberman; she hired a new trainer, Jim Breedlove, changed her lucky socks, and made an increased commitment to her already spartan training regimen.

Going into Wimbledon, Navratilova's losing streak remained unbroken, but she had always had a special affinity for this particular tournament. Its charm held for her in 1987. She sailed through the opening rounds, ousted Evert in the semifinals, and beat the fast-rising Graf in the finals. The victory was her sixth straight Wimbledon championship, eclipsing the all-time record held by the great Suzanne Lenglen. Her eighth overall Wimbledon singles championship, it allowed her to tie the record held by Helen Wills Moody. "How many more do you want?" Graf asked her afterward while extending congratulations. "Nine is my lucky number," she replied. She then went on to prove that the sporting obituaries prepared for her were premature by winning the U.S. Open for the fourth time.

Even when she struggled, as would now be inevitable on some occasions, she remained a crowd favorite. "Like Billie Jean King," observed Olga Morozova, coach of the Soviet women's team, "Martina

By 1990, Navratilova was twice the age of some of her competitors on the women's tour, including 14-year-old Jennifer Capriati (at left), with whom she was photographed in an easygoing moment before the start of that year's Eastbourne Championships. Inspired by Navratilova, Capriati and slightly more mature competitors, such as Arantxa Sanchez (right), had brought a new level of athleticism to the women's game.

not only gave strength to the sport, she gave music also. [She] gave art to the tennis. Now [among the younger players] it's hit hit hit—and less thinking." Her coaches and trainers marveled at the degree of pain she was willing to endure in order to remain on track and on top. Tim Gulliksen received a call from Navratilova in the summer of 1988, right after she had failed in her first try for the ninth Wimbledon title. She summoned him to Texas for a two-week stint of intensive workouts in order to prepare for the U.S. Open. "Fort Worth was in the grip of a heat wave," Gulliksen recalled in an interview with *Tennis* magazine, but Navratilova was undaunted. "We did hard drills six days a week in sessions that lasted from 10 A.M. to 3:30 P.M. It was on a hard court that got so hot our sweat sizzled when it hit the surface. Three days a week Martina did weight training and three days, she did workouts on the track, mostly sprints and middle-distance runs. At the end of almost every day, we played ninety minutes of two-on-two basketball."

This time, however, as would become more commonplace, there was no gain for the pain. Navratilova lost in the quarterfinals of the 1988 U.S. Open. Her computer ranking dropped to number two, and she reorganized Team Navratilova yet again, enlisting help from a sports psychologist, Dr. James Loehr, and coaching input from Billie Jean King and Craig Kardon.

Throughout this period of reassessment, Nelson had been a mainstay. The couple spent most of their free time making plans to move from Fort Worth to Aspen, where they intended to build their dream house—a unique 7,000-square-foot home of stucco and glass on 100 acres of land, with an indoor lap pool, a barn for seven horses, and a garage for seven cars. They looked forward to being surrounded there by other tennis players who enjoyed working out in the pristine mountain air and to living in a place that was used to celebrities.

Nineteen ninety proved to be a momentous year for Navratilova. Undoubtedly, the high point was the record-breaking ninth Wimbledon title, achieved by defeating Zina Garrison in the finals. "Nothing I'll ever do in sports will top this," she said afterward. "Nothing. I've waited a long time for this—I always knew I had one more Wimbledon in me even though a lot of people didn't think I did." At the awards ceremony, the Duchess of Kent, who presents the Wimbledon trophy each year, put aside protocol by pushing the weeping Navratilova's outstretched hand aside and kissing her on both cheeks.

Wanting to share the moment with the person who had been through it all with her, Navratilova made that daring climb through the stands to embrace Nelson. Later, the couple celebrated at a London restaurant with friends, including Evert and King.

But the good times that Navratilova and Nelson had shared together were coming to an end. Navratilova was knocked out of the U.S. Open in the first round, and knee surgery in December halted her season. More important to the couple, by the New Year of 1991, Navratilova had decided that she had fallen out of love with Nelson.

Friends had noticed for some time that Navratilova seemed restless in the relationship. There were tensions over the distribution of profits from the couple's joint business venture, MN Sportswear, and Navratilova seemed to be paying a lot of attention to a new friend, ski instructor Cindy Nelson. The move to Aspen had changed things between the two, and while Nelson believed the couple was just going through a rough patch that they would be able to work out, Navratilova was moving away. In Fort Worth, the two had stood together as the odd couple in a standoffish, straight, sometimes hostile community, but Aspen was host to a constant parade of sophisticated celebrities among whom Navratilova mingled freely as a star in her own right. Perhaps for the first time, she began to regard life as a single woman as not undesirable, and she began to feel stifled by the assumption of monogamy on which her relationship with Nelson was based. As was her pattern, Navratilova had reached a point where she experienced her current partner as holding her back from some ostensibly more fulfilling part of her life.

Just after the New Year, Judy and Martina had a confrontation about the nature of Navratilova's relationship with Cindy Nelson. In the course of a melodramatic evening of confessions, ultimatums, and lots of crying, Navratilova grabbed her suitcase, her tennis racket, and her skis, packed them into her red Ford Explorer, and drove away. Judy expected that, after taking some time to cool off, Navratilova would return, but she never did.

With the exception of Rita Mae Brown, the women in Navratilova's life had all made significant sacrifices in their own lives and careers to be with her on a full-time basis. In return for their devotion, Navratilova loved them and made them feel important. She put her trust in them and depended on them—and she paid the bills. She made possible a charmed way of life, one that included lavish homes, travel, the best restaurants, and relatively unrestricted access to her assets.

In her autobiography, Nancy Lieberman gave the following example by way of trying to explain how compelling it was to be the object of Navratilova's affection: "In 1981, Martina and I were walking down Wilshire Boulevard [in Los Angeles] when a hot car blew by, and I asked Martina what kind it was. She told me it was a Ferrari. I said something like, 'That is a really hot looking car.' Her response was, 'Nancy, here is my credit card. The Ferrari place is two blocks down the street on the right. Go down there and test drive one, and if you like it, just go ahead and get it.'"

For whatever combination of emotional and material reasons, it was never Navratilova's companion who chose to end the relationship. She always did the leaving. And when she left, she left abruptly, demonstrating an unnerving capacity to sever emotional bonds overnight and move on. According to Lieberman, "When Martina has enough of something, she is like, 'That's it. I'm out of here. Period.' She doesn't realize that she is hurting people, tearing them apart. It's not like she means to hurt people, but she can hurt them unwittingly and then go on with her life without skipping a beat." In her introduction to Faulkner's book, Rita Mae Brown confirms Lieberman's description of Martina's method of leavetaking. "Martina subscribes to the Mario Andretti school of departure—put the pedal to the metal and get the hell out of Dodge," Brown wrote.

In the wake of each breakup, Navratilova's companions each seemed to feel that they were owed something. Perhaps they felt this because

Navratilova fights back tears after winning her record ninth Wimbledon singles title in 1990. That number includes six straight championships from 1982 to 1987.

being with her was demanding and it required that they give up a part of themselves; perhaps they felt that without her they could not continue living the lifestyle to which they had become accustomed; or perhaps they wanted her to pay for the pain that is caused by being left so abruptly. For her part, the unembittered Navratilova usually responded generously, and it was her practice to provide her former companions with large financial settlements. Brown got to keep the 26-room Charlottesville mansion, which was completely paid for, and she also received an undisclosed amount of money. Lieberman was given $72,000.

Navratilova fully intended to negotiate a financial settlement with Nelson as well. According to Faulkner, she was prepared to negotiate a division of the three houses they owned in Aspen, their partnership in MN Sportswear, and custody of their pets. Beyond that, she anticipated paying Nelson something in the neighborhood of $30,000 for each year they had been together.

Nelson, however, rejected these tentative offers. "I want what is in the agreement," Faulkner quotes her as saying.

The agreement, of course, referred to the nonmarital cohabitation document the couple had signed in 1986. By its terms, Nelson was legally entitled to half of Navratilova's earnings since 1984, a total of somewhere between three and five million dollars. By Nelson's reasoning, she was entitled to such a sum because the two were equal partners in "Martina"—a diverse financial conglomerate of accumulated prize money, bonus money, compensation for exhibitions and product endorsements, profits from their business venture, returns on investments, real estate, and savings accounts. As Nelson saw it, she had given up her previous security in life as a doctor's wife and independent businesswoman—a considerable sacrifice—in order to devote herself full time to Navratilova. If their lives were of equal worth, and both women had devoted themselves to building "Martina," then Nelson reckoned that half of "Martina" belonged to her. "For seven years," she told journalists at a press conference, "I have assisted and supported Martina, and I have sacrificed my personal goals in the process. Both Martina and I wanted an agreement which reflected the commitment that was made and which underscored the financial responsibilities we assumed for each other. . . . I changed directions in my life, and I would say at some risk. I took on a new relationship and a new way of life. I don't think people can understand it unless it happened to them."

When Navratilova's argument that the agreement was not binding failed to convince Nelson to drop her demands, she advised IGM, her managing agency, to cancel Nelson's access to the "benefits" she was still providing—credit cards, health and car insurance, and their mutual savings and checking accounts. As required by their agreement, she then sent Nelson a letter formally dissolving their relationship. At an impasse, the two called in Rita Mae Brown in the hope that she could mediate the dispute. In an interview, Brown said that had Martina just given the money she would end up spending on attorney's fees, "she could have solved the whole mess in approximately thirty minutes, but pride goeth . . . ." When Brown's efforts failed, the battling former lovers called their attorneys.

With the media reporting on every development, the Nelson-Navratilova "love match," as it was dubbed, made its way into court. Nelson officially filed her suit in early June 1991, just before Wimbledon, seemingly as a means of harassing her former lover and ensuring herself maximum publicity at a time when Navratilova was sure to be in the news anyway. Navratilova's attorney, Mike McCurley, succeeded in gaining a postponement until September, affording Navratilova the opportunity, in late July, to publicly present her side of the story in the forum of an interview with television journalist Barbara Walters on the program "20/20."

Navratilova told the viewing audience that the agreement had been made in order to protect Nelson's rights to her estate in the event of an accident or illness. In states that do not acknowledge gay or domestic partnerships, couples must explicitly assign rights and property to each other to ensure that members of their biological families do not make decisions or claims to property or inheritance that exclude the partner. Without some document to this effect, the rights of blood relatives—no matter how distant and estranged—will supercede the rights of a gay partner.

Furthermore, Navratilova explained, she had been deceived about the agreement's terms. She expected that the agreement was going to be based on the three pages of handwritten notes that she had given to BeAnn Sisemore, in which she indicated that Nelson was to receive 50 percent of their joint business earnings and $30,000 for every year they were together, a sum that was far less than half of her earnings. Instead, she was presented with a typed 14-page agreement containing quite different terms. "I was thinking to myself, this is not what I thought it was," Navratilova explained, "but you know I didn't want to make waves. . . . I trusted everyone." Though she admitted that she read the agreement ("but not carefully"), initialed every page, and waived her right to consult an attorney, she now told Walters that she believed she had been "tricked," made the victim of a plan that was "organized pretty much ahead of time. . . . [Judy] figured that she was either going to have me or have a lot of money. . . . My crime here is stupidity, naïveté and not loving Judy anymore. For that I have to pay."

But the most significant thing about the interview was not the allegations Navratilova made about the lawsuit, but that she had spoken clearly and unequivocally, on national television, about her sexuality. "Well, obviously, the only reason why there was any agreement," she said, looking straight into the camera, "was because we had a relationship. We lived as man and wife: two women living together, loving each other." These words represented a kind of historic reclamation: ten years earlier, while speaking to Walters on national television, Billie Jean King had been unable to be so straightforward. While some feminists cringed at Navratilova's use of the phrase "man and wife" to describe a relationship between two women, gay rights activists rejoiced at its explicitness and her visibility: this famous, successful, glamorous woman, "20/20" reported to the world, lived with, slept with, and had sex with another woman. In this instant, Navratilova became "political." She not only lived within the truth, she had given the truth a human form and a voice—on prime-time television, no less. She became the Martina who made it all right to be gay.

Navratilova's argument was no defense in court, however; as Walters had pointed out again and again, she had signed the agreement, and she

The September 1991 court proceedings to resolve Navratilova's legal dispute with Judy Nelson were emotionally wrenching for all parties involved.

knew what she was signing. In court, her case centered on the enforceability of the contract under Texas law and whether Nelson's attorney, Jerry Loftin, had the right to represent her in this matter, as he had been representing Navratilova at the time the agreement was signed, and Sisemore had been his employee.

On the first day of the hearing in Fort Worth, emotions outweighed legal technicalities. Nelson and Navratilova were in the same room together for the first time since April. Nelson's parents, who were present, hugged Navratilova upon seeing her. Eddie and Bales Nelson were also in attendance, a reminder to Navratilova, no doubt, of the letters each had written her after the breakup, expressing their love for her and the hope that she and their mother would reconcile. Navratilova had not answered. With Sisemore fainting from exhaustion and the tension of having to justify her part in this dispute, Navratilova crying on the stand, and Nelson sobbing at the lawyers' table, the proceedings, reported one journalist, were a "three-hanky affair."

"It was the worst day of my life," Nelson said afterward. Not surprisingly, the emotionally exhausting day spurred both parties' interest in a settlement. After some more sparring, a settlement was reached. Nelson received the smallest of the three houses in Colorado as well as a cash payment—a package worth slightly more than a million dollars. She also retained the right to publish a book about their relationship. In exchange, she agreed not to contest Navratilova's claim that the agreement they had signed was not valid. This provided Navratilova with a basis for her case against Loftin, whom she was now suing for damages and the cost of all her legal fees in connection with the suit.

Another outcome of the case provided a somewhat comical sense of closure: Judy Nelson and Rita Mae Brown became a couple. "Well, [that's] strange," Navratilova said to writer Michele Kort in 1993 about the new arrangement. "That's never happened to me before. But I think those two deserve each other."

When Brown was interviewed in 1994, she referred to Nelson as a "friend" and expressed concern that the end of the Nelson-Navratilova love match had cost the tennis star more than money:

> Martina tired of Judy, I can understand that, but Judy was a stable factor in her life and once removed Martina has not been as successful. It isn't just age because she's a strong woman, physically. She's lost it. Maybe she could have worked things out with Judy but I'm not sure she tried.
>
> It worries me that she's adrift and I believe that Judy Nelson still loves her and would again join forces with her and provide a rudder to the ship, so to speak. Martina could do a whole lot worse.

CHAPTER TWELVE

MARTINA JOINS THE MOVEMENT

For Navratilova, the breakup of a relationship had often signaled that she was about to "remake" herself in some significant way. But while some predicted that the strain of the lawsuit with Nelson would hasten her exit from professional tennis, in 1992 Navratilova and her reconstructed knee played a full schedule on the circuit. She was much less successful, however, than in the past, reaching the finals of just four tournaments and winning just one. She remained committed to competing, however. "I'll be there," she testily told a writer for *Sports Illustrated* who suggested that there might not be a next year. "If you don't see me, it's because you didn't show up."

Change was more evident in her personal life, but not in the way that might have been expected. In the past, Navratilova had gone from one intense relationship right into another, but now, she said, she had learned to "take things slowly." To deal with the emotional fallout from the end of the relationship

Wearing her trademark "statement" shorts, Navratilova returns a shot in a 1993 match.

with Nelson, she entered psychotherapy. Nelson "really threw me for a loop and I really had to deal with that," she told Michele Kort in an interview for the *Advocate*. "I've done major personal growth in the last year. I've been single for the first time and I've really spent time on my own. . . . Wish I had done it sooner. It's given me a much better balance as a human and as an athlete, but maybe that's taken that edge off the tennis, because it's not the only thing in my life. And it shouldn't be. . . . I'm seeing somebody, but I'm taking things slowly. In the past it was 'Let's get married tomorrow.' I've learned."

One consequence, perhaps, of achieving the "better balance" that she spoke about was a noticeable shift in the way Navratilova handled references to her sexual orientation. She no longer used the term "bisexual" and seemed less wedded to her previous conviction that being gay could or should remain an entirely private matter. As experts on lesbian and gay identity note, "coming out" is not a single act but a lifelong process. Perhaps for Navratilova, the lawsuit, which on one level was an unwanted, embarrassing, and painful revelation of the details of her personal life, also provided an opportunity to take another step in the process of coming out.

Navratilova's statements about her sexuality on "20/20" had brought forth a barrage of requests for endorsements and appearances at events supporting gay rights. While it is seldom the case that declaring one's identity as lesbian or gay translates into social movement participation, Navratilova became an exception. In the past, Navratilova had devoted time and money to organizations that worked with inner-city children and welfare mothers. However, in contrast to charitable giving to less fortunate groups to which she herself did not belong, Navratilova's direct participation in the gay rights movement meant something more. It resonated with the passion of her own personal experience—of growing up gay, of suffering discrimination in her profession, of having her citizenship threatened, and of dealing with friends who patronized her. "I'm gay and I won't live a lie, she wrote in a guest editorial for *USA Today*.

Her involvement in the world of political protest began in her own backyard in Aspen, Colorado. Navratilova had initially chosen to reside in Colorado because of its reputation for political and cultural tolerance, but in November 1992 the state legislature passed Amendment 2, which repealed existing gay rights laws in the cities of Denver, Boulder, and Aspen and prohibited the outlawing of discrimination based on sexual preference. Up to this point, Navratilova told the *Advocate,* "I'd been out, but I hadn't been waving the flag. . . . I sort of got thrown into the spotlight. . . . All of a sudden everyone wanted to talk to me. All of a sudden I'm this expert on gay rights."

To prevent enforcement of the law, the ACLU filed a lawsuit on behalf of the cities of Denver, Boulder, and Aspen and the lesbians, gay men, and bisexuals of the state of Colorado. Nine lesbians, gay men, and bisexuals joined the suit as individual plaintiffs, claiming that Amendment 2 denied them their First Amendment and Fourteenth Amendment rights of free speech, association, and equal protection under the law. Among the nine was Navratilova.

Her stated reasons for joining the suit related not only to being gay and a resident of Colorado but to her experience as a political exile. "My happy life in Czechoslovakia changed drastically when the Communists took over in 1968," she wrote in the *USA Today* editorial. "I swore then that I would never take any rights or citizenship for granted." When she applied for U.S. citizenship, she explained, she believed that the Declaration of Independence and the Constitution guaranteed that what happened to her in Czechoslovakia could never happen again. "I never dreamed that years later, in my adopted home state of Colorado, my life would be threatened by an amendment that is contrary to all I learned about U.S. citizenship." In *Ladies Home Journal,* she was equally eloquent in rebutting the opposition's argument that in opposing Amendment 2, gays were seeking "special rights."

"We are not asking for special rights," Navratilova said, "we are asking for equality, for the same rights everyone else has under the Constitution: the right not to be dismissed from a job or to be denied housing simply because of who we are. Now, under Amendment 2, we are denied those rights." She repeatedly announced her intention to move out of Colorado if Amendment 2 was not overturned. "I will not pay taxes in a state that does not recognize me as an equal citizen," she said.

The economic approach was also seized on by numerous gay rights organizations, including the Gay and Lesbian Association Against Defamation (GLAAD) and the National Lesbian and Gay Task Force, which called upon "all the citizens of the United States and of the world to boycott Colorado as a destination for business or recreational purposes and to boycott all products originating in the state." The proposed boycott was aimed especially at the state's lucrative tourism industry and became a high-profile issue when a straight supporter of gay rights, singer, actress, and filmmaker Barbra Streisand, called upon her celebrity colleagues, many of whom wintered in the ski resorts of Aspen and Vail, to honor the ban.

Navratilova, however, outspokenly disagreed with this strategy, believing that a boycott would inflict unfair economic punishment on Boulder, Denver, and Aspen, whose pro-gay policies had inspired the reactionary Amendment 2 in the first place. While many prominent organizations, such as the National Education Association and the American Association of Physicians for Human Rights, canceled their plans to hold conventions in Colorado in 1993, the media focused on the "to ski or not to ski" debate among Hollywood celebrities, to the chagrin of grassroots activists who felt that the real issue was being trivialized.

At the same time, the supporters of the amendment, primarily the members of a right-wing coalition called "Coloradans for Family Values," remained adamant. "The message to you from Colorado is clear," wrote Ken Bonetti, a resident of the conservative city of Ft. Collins. "We don't want the National Education Association nor any other group that is sympathetic to homosexuality holding a convention in our state. We don't want the Martina Navratilovas here flaunting their lifestyle in front of our children. We don't need Barbra Streisands as tourists. We don't want businesses and organizations tolerant of homosexual acts and other abominations relocating in Colorado."

Meanwhile, Navratilova used every venue available to her to keep the issue alive, making numerous public appearances, going on the

The end of her playing career may mean increased visibility for Navratilova as an activist. Here, she wears a T-shirt designed for Pridefest, a gay pride celebration held in Philadelphia in May 1994

television programs "Nightline" and "Good Morning America," and even using the Virginia Slims tournament as a forum. "Throughout the tournament," *Sports Illustrated* noted, "Navratilova was a walking paid political announcement. She lectured tirelessly on Colorado's Amendment 2." As the Colorado lawsuit entered Denver's District Court, she was recruited by the National Lesbian and Gay Task Force to sign a fund-raising letter that solicited support for the "Campaign To End the Ban on Gays in the Military." When the White House settled on a compromise "no see, no tell" policy concerning gays in the military, Navratilova criticized President Bill Clinton on national television for not fulfilling his promise to end the ban.

Navratilova was equally outspoken in responding to the announcement that professional basketball star Earvin "Magic" Johnson had tested positive for the HIV virus, which causes AIDS. As she explained to a

New York Post reporter, she believed that the largely sympathetic response that Johnson received was because he was a man who supposedly contracted the disease through sexual encounters with many different women. People would be much less understanding, she said, if she announced that she had the virus. "They'd say I'm gay and I deserved to get it. . . . If it had happened to a heterosexual woman who had been with 100 or 200 men, they'd call her a whore and a slut and the corporations would drop her like a lead balloon." She added that she meant no offense to Johnson, whom she had met and liked, "but the double standard is there, it's scary, and it makes me mad as hell."

Navratilova's career as a gay rights activist reached its high point in April 1993, when she addressed an estimated audience of 500,000 people at the Lesbian and Gay March on Washington, the largest gay pride rally ever. When the MC introduced Navratilova, the crowd did not even wait for her to appear on the stage: they broke loose in a standing ovation and a sustained roar. "It was as if nothing Navratilova could go on to say could be more eloquent than the way she conducted her public life," observed a *Washington Post* reporter.

Looking very butch in a yellow T-shirt, black Dockers, and a Western belt, Navratilova stood before the podium and announced, "I'm not going to cry." She shook her finger at the audience: "Don't you even think about it." And then she delivered her speech, which was interrupted by applause no less than six times:

> What our movement for equality needs most, in my not-so-humble opinion, is for us to come out of the closet. We need to become visible to as many people as possible, so that we can finally shatter all those incredible myths that help keep us in the closet.
>
> Let's come out and let all the people see what, for the most part, straight and square and normal and sometimes boring lives we lead. Let's come out and dispel the rumors and lies that are being spread about us. Let's come out and set everybody straight, so to speak.
>
> Our goal is not to receive compassion, acceptance, or worse yet, tolerance, because that implies that we are inferior, we are able to be tolerated, pitied, endured. I don't want pity, do you?

Of course not! Our goal must be equality across the board. We can settle for nothing less, because we deserve nothing less.

One's sexuality should not be an issue, one way or another. One's sexuality should not become a label by which that human being should be identified. My sexuality is a very important part of my being, but it is still a very small part of my makeup, a very small part of what creates a whole human being. In any case being a lesbian is not an accomplishment. It is not something I had to learn, study for, or graduate in.

It is what I am. Nothing more, nothing less.

Now I did not spend over thirty years of my life working my butt off trying to become the very best tennis player that I can be, to then be called Martina, the lesbian tennis player. Labels are for filing, labels are bookkeeping, labels are for clothing. Labels are not for people.

Being homosexual, bisexual, or heterosexual is not good or bad. It simply is.

"I was a wreck doing the speech," Navratilova later told the *Advocate*, "but I wanted to be a part of it. It was unbelievable. I would have paid to have been there."

But in time, Navratilova's enthusiasm for political activism seemed to wane. She was guest of honor at a fund-raising dinner and auction to benefit Gay Games IV, where one of her tennis rackets, a personal lesson, and dinner with her fetched a bid of $30,000, but by the fall of 1993 she was keeping a much lower political profile. By the time the Amendment 2 lawsuit was decided in favor of the plaintiffs in October, she had removed her name, citing her commitments on the tennis circuit. She also declined an invitation to make an appearance, even via videotape, at the opening ceremonies for Gay Games IV, which were held in New York City in June 1994. In an interview, Rita Mae Brown offered an explanation for Navratilova's shifting level of political commitment:

> The gay movement had little impact on Martina until the end of her career. Considering the years she consciously distanced herself from gay issues, I think this sudden embrace by gay movement leaders is quite remarkable. Shall I assume they are a highly evolved and forgiving lot, or shall I wonder who is exploiting whom? . . . She [Martina] is not a person motivated by causes unless it is in her self-interest to be involved or if she gets a lot of applause.

That's what makes her so great on the court. . . . It's unfair to expect too much of her. If she prevaricates or chickens out, just ask yourself how many politicos can hit that kind of forehand. . . . It all evens out.

This shift in emphasis was accompanied by an enormous change in her life, the greatest she had undergone since deciding to leave Czechoslovakia. In September 1993, looking pensive and composed, Navratilova announced at a press conference in New York that 1994 would be her last year of competitive singles play. "I've been in the twilight of my career longer than most people have had their career," she said. "I'm No. 3 in the world and I want the chance to retire on my own terms."

But for most of her final season, Navratilova's performance fell far short of her own standards. Though she made it to the finals of the Italian Open and the Pan Pacific Tournament in Tokyo, she lost to the player ranked 231st in the world at the Virginia Slims tournament in

A farewell wave: Navratilova exits Wimbledon after making her final appearance there as a player in July 1994.

Houston. At the French Open, she smashed her racket into a chair after dropping her opening-round match.

Anyone who had followed Navratilova's career would have known that if there was going to be a fairy-tale ending, it would come at Wimbledon. She cruised through the opening rounds, then ousted Jana Novotna in the quarterfinals and Helena Sukova in the semifinals. At her 22nd Wimbledon, Navratilova was making her twelfth trip to the finals. "I'm like a bad dream that keeps coming back," she joked. "Or a good dream, depending on whether you want me to be here or not."

Judging by the way the crowds responded to her, most of those in attendance very much wanted Navratilova to be there. In the finals, wearing her "statement shorts," her racket adorned with a pink triangle (a symbol of gay pride), she played well but nonetheless lost to 22-year-old Conchita Martinez in three sets. At the closing ceremony, as she engaged in a tearful exchange with the Duchess of Kent, she was treated to an extended standing ovation. As she returned to Centre Court to grab a handful of grass as a souvenir, shouts of "We love you, Martina" rang out. "Is this goodbye?" Bud Collins asked after the ceremony. "Definitely," she answered, willing herself to smile through the tears streaming down her face.

To this point, Navratilova has only speculated about her future. She has mentioned the possibility of doing a television series. She has signed a contract to coauthor three mystery novels set in the world of professional tennis. She has stated her intention to continue as an activist on such issues as gay rights, the environment, and women's issues. She has considered having a child, through artificial insemination, and she sometimes fantasizes about "doing nothing" or "going somewhere where I don't know anybody and nobody knows me."

If indeed the future is made of the same stuff as the past, then it seems certain that Navratilova will fashion a "next life" that is well worth watching. At the age of 38, she is a woman of tremendous resources. In addition to the great athletic skills that have made her enormously wealthy, she possesses a keen intelligence, a wry sense of humor, and little fear of controversy or speaking her mind. Having already invented her own life not just as a tennis player, but as a woman, as an American, and as a lesbian, Navratilova is certainly equipped to create a meaningful existence for herself outside the narrow world of professional athletics.

But even should all her most meaningful accomplishments be behind her, Navratilova has left an inspiring legacy. In 22 years on the international tennis circuit, Navratilova has rewritten the record book in a way no player before her—male or female—had ever done. She transformed sports for women by taking on the training discipline of men. She broke with the tradition of women's tennis that had a player guided by a father or male coach by creating Team Navratilova, which always had a woman at the helm. She did not allow competition to interfere with friendship, or sports or governments to dictate decisions made about her personal life. To men she was an athlete they could respect on their own terms—competitive, aggressive, driven. To women, she represented the unbridled, undomesticated parts of themselves. To lesbians and gays she made coming out a lot easier.

And she always permitted others to witness her struggle, to see her passion and vulnerability, the shining moments and the unshining ones, the sleek, graceful Martina and Navrat the brat, stamping her feet and crying beneath a towel, the courageous activist, thoughtful spokesperson, and generous friend and the self-absorbed athlete and impetuous lover. By observing someone who displayed both a sense of invincibility and fragility, we learned to accept these completely human contradictions in ourselves and in others. It is in this sense that so many derived inspiration from Martina Navratilova.

FURTHER READING

Brown, Rita Mae. *Rubyfruit Jungle*. NY: Bantam, 1988.

Faulkner, Sandra. *Love Match: Nelson vs. Navratilova*. New York: Birch Lane Press, 1993.

Feinstein, John. *Hard Courts*. NY: Villard, 1992.

King, Billie Jean. *We Have Come a Long Way*. NY: McGraw, 1988.

King, Billie Jean, with Frank Deford. *Billie Jean*. New York: Viking, 1982.

Lichtenstein, Grace. *Long Way, Baby*. NY: William Morris, 1974.

Lieberman, Nancy, with Nancy Jennings. *Lady Magic*. Champaign, IL: Sagamore, 1992.

Mandlikova, Hana, with Michael Folley. *Hana*. London: Barker, 1989.

Navratilova, Martina, with Mary Carillo. *Tennis My Way: A Complete Guide to Training & Playing*. NY: Penguin, 1984.

Navratilova, Martina, with George Vecsey. *Martina: An Autobiography*. New York: Knopf, 1985.

Nelson, Mariah Burton. *Are We Winning Yet? How Women Are Changing Sports and Sports Are Changing Women*. New York: Random House, 1991.

Richards, Renée, and John Ames. *Second Serve*. Briarcliff Manor, NY: Stein & Day, 1983.

Shriver, Pam, et al. *Passing Shots*. NY: McGraw, 1988.

Stabiner, Karen. *Courting Fame: The Perilous Road to Women's Tennis Stardom*. NY: Harper and Row, 1986.

Young, Perry Deane. *Lesbians and Gays and Sports*. New York: Chelsea House, 1995.

CHRONOLOGY

1956   Born Martina Subertova on October 18 in Prague, Czechoslovakia

1964   Enters her first junior tennis tournament and makes the semifinals

1966   Changes name to Navratilova after her stepfather adopts her

1968   Soviet occupation of Czechoslovakia

1969   Allowed to leave Czechoslovakia for the first time on a tennis exchange with West Germany

1973   Wins first "adult" title, the Czechoslovakia National Championship; begins competing in the United States

1975   Defects to the United States

1978   Wins French Open; defeats Chris Evert to capture Wimbledon title; ranked number one in the world by Women's Tennis Association

1979   Wins Wimbledon as her mother cheers in the stands; begins relationship with Rita Mae Brown

1981   Receives U.S. citizenship; meets Nancy Lieberman; hires Renée Richards as her coach

1982   Sweeps the Australian Open, the French Open, and Wimbledon; regains number-one ranking

1983   Wins Wimbledon; finally achieves U.S. Open victory; named Associated Press Female Athlete of the Year

1984   Ends partnership with Lieberman; marries Judy Nelson

1985   Writes *Martina: An Autobiography* with George Vecsey

1986   Wracks up seventh Wimbledon championship; achieves third U.S. Open victory; returns to Czechoslovakia as member of U.S. team in Federation Cup tournament

1987	Wins a record sixth straight victory at Wimbledon (eighth overall); records fourth U.S. Open win
1990	Defeats Zina Garrison for a record ninth Wimbledon championship; officially restored to personhood by Czech government
1991	Breaks up with Judy Nelson; formally comes out on nationally broadcast Barbara Walters interview; reaches financial settlement with Nelson
1992	Assumes role in gay rights movement; campaigns against Colorado's discriminatory Amendment 2
1993	Makes waves at Wimbledon by playing in shorts instead of a tennis skirt; speaks before crowd of 500,000 at Lesbian and Gay March on Washington; announces that 1994 will be her last year of competitive singles play
1994	Bids emotional farewell to Wimbledon by reaching finals for the twelfth time; honored at Virginia Slims tournament in New York City

INDEX

Gilda Zwerman is Associate Professor of Sociology at the State University of New York at Old Westbury and a psychotherapist in New York City. She is the author of *Mothering on the Lam: Women and Political Violence in the United States,* Basic Books, 1996.

Martin Duberman is Distinguished Professor of History at the Graduate Center for the City University of New York and the founder and director of the Center for Gay and Lesbian Studies. One of the country's foremost historians, he is the author of 15 books and numerous articles and essays. He has won the Bancroft Prize for *Charles Francis Adams* (1960); two Lambda awards for *Hidden from History: Reclaiming the Gay and Lesbian Past,* an anthology that he coedited; and a special award from the National Academy of Arts and Letters for his overall "contributions to literature." His play *In White America* won the Vernon Rice/Drama Desk Award in 1964. His other works include *James Russell Lowell* (1966), *Black Mountain: An Exploration in Community* (1972), *Paul Robeson* (1989), *Cures: A Gay Man's Odyssey* (1991), and *Stonewall* (1993).

Professor Duberman received his Ph.D. in history from Harvard University in 1957 and served as professor of history at Yale University and Princeton University from 1957 until 1972, when he assumed his present position at the City University of New York.

ACKNOWLEDGMENTS

This biography was written almost exclusively from secondary sources, the most important of which were *Martina: An Autobiography* by George Vecsey (with Martina Navratilova) and *Love Match: Nelson vs. Navratilova* by Sandra Faulkner (with Judy Nelson).

I wish to thank the following people who took the time to explain some aspect of Martina Navratilova's life and career to me: George Vecsey, Dr. Marge Snyder, Yolanda Jackson, Nancy Zimbalist, Nancy Solomon, Rita Mae Brown, Dr. James Loehr, Michele Kort, Amy Connelly, Grace Lichtenstein, and Ana Leaird.

Many thanks also to those who provided personal support during completion of this manuscript: Justin Trager, Lisa Trager, Polly Thistlewaite, Morton Sobell, Nancy Gruber, Margaret Nash, Elaine Scott, Harry Scott, Barbara Joseph, Jeffrey Escoffier, Nancy Bereano, Rosalyn Baxandall, Eve Rosahn, Jonathan Rabinovitz, Sharon Thompson, Gil Zicklin, Dora Ierides and the Clark Center crew, my trusted and trusty secretary, Regina Rudowski, and my students in the 1993–94 Sociological Theory class at the College at Old Westbury.

Very special thanks to companions and hand-holders Jan Oxenberg and Billy Bird-Forteza.

Research materials used in this work will be donated to the Lesbian Herstory Archives and the Women's Sports Foundation.

DEDICATION

This book is dedicated in memory of my friends Vito Russo and Martin Levine.